Teaching
Preschool
Reading

All photographs are courtesy of the Montessori Children's House, Council Bluffs, Iowa, Dorothy A. Woods and Irene Dawson, Directresses. All photos by Bob Pyles Studio, Council Bluffs, Iowa.

Teaching Preschool Reading

Sandra Harvey Heater

Brigham Young University Press

Library of Congress Cataloging in Publication Data

Heater, Sandra Harvey, 1942-
    Teaching preschool reading.

    Bibliography: p. 105
    1. Reading (Preschool)   I. Title.
LB1140.5.R4H4   372.4'1   80-18768
ISBN 0-8425-1837-1

Library of Congress Catalog Card Number: 80-18768
International Standard Book Number: 0-8425-1837-1
Brigham Young University Press, Provo, Utah 84602
© 1980 Brigham Young University Press. All rights reserved
Printed in the United States of America
10/80   47088

Contents

Preface   vii

Introduction   1

1. Nurturing Early Language Development   9
   Visual and Audio Stimulation   9
   Conversation—Speak English!   12
   TV as a Teacher   13
   Other Sensory Opportunities   14
   Books and More Books   15
   Speak the Speech Properly   18
   Other Readiness Activities   21
   Selecting Toys   25
   Do It Yourself   26

2. The Montessori Way   31
   Phonics? Review!   33
   Readiness Checklist   34
   Select the Best Time and Place   35
   Do We Group?   37

3. Presentation of Material   49
   Tracing the Sandpaper Letters   49

Using the Sound Boxes   52
Practicing with the Mystery Bag   53
Using the Sound Cards   54
Second-Week Activities   56
Presenting Vowels   56
Teaching with a Calendar   59
On to Phonograms   60
Movable Alphabet   64
Blends and Digraphs   67
Look, Say—No Way!   72
Building Word Endings   76
Vary Activities   78

4. Where to Go from Here   79
Checklists   81
Nursery Schools   84

5. Implications of Early Reading   89

6. To the Teacher   97
Sandpaper Letters   98
Oral Reading   98
Show and Tell Variations   99
Educational Games   99
What about the Early Reader?   102
Still More Activities   103

References   105

Suggested Reading   107

Appendixes   111

1. Montessori Exercises   111
2. Time Tables for Speech Sounds   117
3. Manufacturers of Stimulating Toys   118
4. Components of a Prepared Environment   120

Preface

As a practicing reading specialist and a former Montessori directress, I am convinced that reading readiness is essential to the reading success of young children.

Certainly I do not think that very early instruction of children is the only answer to preventing reading difficulties; however, consistent, well-designed beginning reading activities are a step toward better reading.

Perhaps one of the richest legacies a parent or teacher can give a child is the love of reading that will open doors to knowledge and pleasure throughout that child's life.

The techniques described in the following pages do work. I can offer numerous examples and documentation.

Use your skill and ingenuity and your interest in children to give them a lasting gift—the ability to read well.

Introduction

Few areas in education evoke more interest than
reading. It is also an area in which disagreement
abounds. In a group of primary teachers one will
encounter advocates of nearly every reading approach,
and such divergency promotes heated arguments. One
will swear by a basal series approach, another will
recommend programmed reading, and a third prefers
Initial Teaching Alphabet (ITA), and on it goes.

Controversy is rampant not only over methodology of
teaching reading but also over the age at which reading
instruction should start. The study of Morphett and
Washburne (1931) emphasized a chronological age of
6½ years that became pretty much accepted as the
beginning point.

Studies have been devoted to proving that children
are not coordinated properly, lack sufficient visual
acuity and perception, have inadequate span of
concentration, and, in general *cannot* and *must* not begin
instruction in reading before the age of six years at the
earliest (Smith and Dechant 1961). Tradition has
played a major role in forming opinion along these

lines. In American schools most children enter first grade within a few months after their sixth birthday, and most of these children *learn to read* to some extent in the first grade.

Sadly enough, all children do not learn to read. For some the reason is a lack of mechanical skills in reading. For others it is emotional problems; occasionally a physical disability results in hampered reading development. The causes may be a combination of these and other factors. The purpose of this book is not to discuss the various conditions that may lead to reading disability. This is a controversial area and is best left to the physicians, psychologists, and reading clinicians.

And we all have seen children whose levels of comprehension are adequate, who have mastered the mechanics of reading, and whose development seems completely normal but who do not *love* reading.

Dr. Maria Montessori said that "a love of reading is every child's natural heritage." She was not speaking of the ability to read but of the *love* of reading. With the importance of reading firmly fixed in the minds of educators, parents, psychologists, and children themselves, what can teachers and parents do to help foster, first, reading readiness and, second, a love of reading?

I know of no pat answers to these complex questions. If only a magic wand would transform all children into competent, joyous readers! Yet this transformation is not possible (though as parents we frequently expect it from our schools).

Today, approaches to reading are exciting. Lately an abundance of new materials and devices have appeared on the market. Publishers of reading series are redesigning their books for children, and never have educators been more aware of the importance of reading to a child's success in school. All these facts should be encouraging to parents, but they must know also that they can and must participate in areas of readiness preparation (Kohl 1973).

The purpose of this book is to explore these possibilities. I hope the reader will finish this volume with an insight into early reading readiness. This book will not transform its public into reading experts; it will not guarantee that every four-year-old will read; and it certainly leaves unanswered many questions in the field of reading. What it will do is explain the Montessori method as it applies strictly to reading. One will find not only numerous suggestions regarding Montessori materials and their manufacture for home use but also suggestions about ways to encourage an early interest in reading and practical ideas for performing reading-readiness tasks with children.

I cannot assure you that this book will teach you to teach your child how to read. What you can expect is to approach reading with your child as a great adventure and to build a solid foundation for his success in reading.

Maria Montessori was the first woman medical doctor in Italy. It was thus not her intention to be an educator, and she shunned any suggestion that she might want to work with children. Yet her work as a physician led her into direct association with children, and with these little ones she made the discoveries that constitute the Montessori method. She was the first to explain that she carried into her work with children no preconceived ideas of an educational system. She did know that she had a deep and true love for children and that she respected them individually and collectively. As Dr. Montessori observed children, she began to realize that certain characteristics are inherent in all children, regardless of race, sex, or nationality.

One of the discoveries Maria Montessori made was

that children have sensitivity periods—stages during which they most readily learn certain activities. She believed that by capitalizing on these sensitivity periods or "periods of discovery," an adult could teach a child certain skills better than at any other time. Maria Montessori therefore designed over 400 didactic (teaching) materials. She placed these materials with the children in a prepared environment.

Astonishing things began to happen to these children in the prepared environment. Children considered scarcely worth the bother "exploded" into writing and into reading. Visitors flocked into the *Casa dei Bambini* (House of Children) to view the results of the Montessori method. People such as Queen Mother Margherita of Savoy; Margaret Wilson, daughter of Woodrow Wilson; Thomas Edison; and Alexander Graham Bell learned of this way of education.

Fortunately, as parents and teachers, we too can create a prepared environment for our children. Of course the prepared environment of Dr. Montessori contained the didactic materials as an important component. However, an atmosphere that nurtures children's curiosity, creativity, and independence also is "prepared."

We can accomplish this by furnishing part of the child's world with child-size equipment, such as chairs and tables that are appropriate to her size. Her closets should have shelves and hooks that are reachable. It is rather senseless to insist that a child hang up her clothes if she cannot reach the clothes hooks. A low, sturdy stepstool provides the little one an opportunity to turn off the lights or to hang up her bath towel. She can thus assume some responsibility for her belongings. We can make numerous physical adjustments, often very slight ones, to allow a child greater control of her surroundings. Challenge your own ingenuity and

The towers provide practice in visual discrimination and eye-hand coordination. Note the prepared environment with the low shelves, rugs, and neatly placed equipment.

powers of observation to see how many modifications you can make to accommodate the physical limitations of young children. (See Appendix 4 for components of a prepared environment.)

As important as the physically suited environment is, even more important is the aesthetic one. It is the harmonious and beautiful environs that truly represent the prepared environment. Surround a child with cleanliness, orderliness, and pleasing sounds and colors, and he will grow up appreciating these qualities in his life. How many of the practical life exercises of Montessori involve cleaning, care of work, precision, and appreciation of beauty!

Each time we play good music, plant flowers, or arrange a bouquet with our child, help him set an

attractive table, encourage him to keep possessions in
their proper places, or use a soft tone of voice, we are
creating a prepared environment. Our own examples of
caring properly for belongings, of stopping to smell the
lilacs, of looking up in wonder at the sky—all these
actions serve to set a learning-and-living stage for our
children.

It has been nearly eighty years since Montessori
became a fixture on the educational scene. Children
from all over the world are in Montessori schools. Since
1958 a resurgence of Montessori schools has occurred,
and many such schools exist in the United States alone.
Her methods are stronger today for the test of time.

However, the purpose of this book is not a history of
the life and work of Maria Montessori. Neither is it a
chronicle of Montessori schools nor the Montessori
technique. The foregoing comments are merely a
prelude to one particular aspect of the Montessori
methodology—reading.

Occasionally we read about a prodigy who taught
herself to read at the age of two. This fills us with a
sense of awe as we consider the usual stage of language
development in a two-year-old. Few children indeed are
that precocious. However, these early years are vital to
the future success of your child's development in every
area. We really cannot afford to leave her language
development to chance any more than we can neglect
her nutritional needs.

Consider for a moment the tremendous growth that
occurs in a baby girl from birth to one year. Not only
have her weight and height increased on a large scale,
but she has changed in twelve short months from a
totally dependent infant into a bundle of well-
coordinated energy. She may well be walking by now,
saying some words, understanding much more than she
can verbally indicate, self-feeding to some extent, and

on down the list of activities for the normal yearling.
Never again will she undergo such a period of physical
growth. In this growth period she has used a year of the
six most important years for all subsequent
development.

Currently early childhood education is in the
spotlight. As parents and teachers we are advised from
all sides on ways to capitalize on these formative early
years. We have learned that 50 percent of a child's
intellectual capacity is reached by the age of four.
Another 30 percent is achieved by age eight. With all
this emphasis on the first six years of life, our
responsibility increases, for a young child spends much
of his time with his parents and much of it with
preschool teachers.

This raises the question of preschools, day-care
centers, nursery schools, working mothers versus "full-
time" mothers, and a host of other questions. This book
will not attempt an answer to these areas of concern,
valid though they are. The subject matter here is
confined to the area of reading.

Let us begin with a few assumptions. The first one is
that you as parents and teachers are vitally interested in
your child's education. The second assumption is that
you will take the necessary time with your children to
develop these areas of reading readiness.

Most adults will answer "yes" readily if asked if they
are interested in and willing to develop their children's
capacities. But this is not enough; an adult must have
sufficient *patience* to work with a child and must be
realistic in expectations.

A three-year-old may ask the same question
repeatedly, but the wise parent or teacher will choke
back the exasperation and answer it carefully as many
times as the child asks the question. However much
time and patience are required, the results are well

worth it all, and the steps along the way toward reading readiness can prove an adventure as exciting as you will ever have.

CHAPTER ONE
Nurturing Early Language Development

You cannot begin reading preparation too early. Parents, before you envision your newborn with book in hand and laugh to yourself, please note that before any child reads, much background must be established. The first-grade teacher does not present your child with a list of words to recognize the first day and thus begin his reading program. This sight list is a part of the reading instruction, but it does not begin there.

Rather the preparation begins in his crib and in your arms. Studies have shown that infants confined primarily to cribs or to very close quarters in one room do not develop as rapidly as infants who are transported in carriers on their mother's backs. Why? One baby is as physically constrained as the other. The answer seems to be that the infant carried about has visual stimulation of a greater variety, and hence he has more opportunity for sensorial exercises than the infant in a crib or room.

Visual and Audio Stimulation

You can begin to provide stimulus for your infant in the bedroom that you arrange for your newborn (Nila 1953).

Father and infant are taking those first important steps to reading.

- Use crib sheets with designs rather than plain ones.

- Place the crib in the middle of the room instead of against the wall.

- Move the crib occasionally to give the baby a new view.

- Hang a mobile above the crib to provide color and motion.

As soon as your baby is old enough to be comfortable in an infant carrier, put the little one in the carrier and let him watch you as you work.

Older children in the same household can serve as teachers for the younger child by playing gently with him. Remember the point of diminishing returns, however. A study of children in large families shows

that when a baby is surrounded by a constant and high
level of noise and confusion, he talks at a later age
(Jennings 1965). Thus you need to strike a balance
between quiet attention and general confusion. Let the
baby watch what the older children do.

As parents you can and should talk to your baby
from the first moment you hold him in your arms.
Granted, he does not understand a word at that point,
and the degree of his hearing acuity is a moot point.
But talking to him is nevertheless invaluable (Jennings
1965). For one thing, a soothing voice is emotionally
satisfying to a newborn, and so is the warmth of the
human touch. He will begin to recognize his mother's
voice by three months or earlier. And long before he can
repeat the words or formulate sentences, he will build a
stockpile of words that have meaning to him.

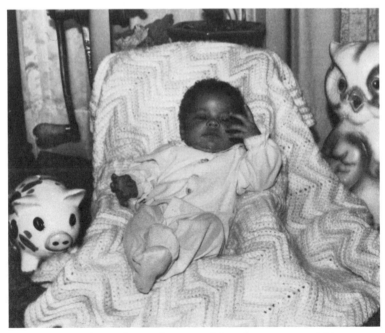

The baby can observe her environment. Note the toys around her.

Conversation—Speak English!

Do not handicap your child with a second language if
that language is baby talk. For some strange reason
adults seem to feel that babies respond better or
comprehend easier these ridiculous mispronunciations
that we foist upon our infants as their language. What
sense does it make for a baby to hear "little"
pronounced as "itty"? One can speak tenderly and
quietly to a baby in standard English as well as in
gibberish.

- Speak as correctly and distinctly to your child as you
  possibly can. Every remark does not have to be a
  lesson in elocution, but you should exercise care in
  your speech. Put yourself in your baby's place by
  attempting to understand a foreign language being
  rapidly and unclearly spoken. Yet we are asking our
  child to do the same thing with what will be his own
  tongue.

  Try to recall an experience when you first used
  successfully your second or "school-book" language.
  The person with whom you talked probably spoke
  more slowly and clearly than he normally would
  when he realized that you were a beginner. How
  pleasant it is to perceive at least a few words of
  another language. How diligently we seek to catch
  words that are meaningful to us.

- Speak to your child in sentences. A few words of his
  own language will not suffice for very long for your
  child. He must come to comprehend and to
  pronounce a great variety of words. These words
  must then become sentences. Inability to use
  language correctly is a big handicap to overcome in a
  child's learning and in his social experiences.

Consider for a moment the way in which we as adults often "talk" to our infants and toddlers. Provided even that we do not use baby talk, the tendency to use single words only is too frequently our habit. Instead of asking our yearling, "Do you want a cookie?" we merely say, "cookie?" The better way is to use the complete sentence and slightly emphasize the stress word. Most of our meaningful communication as adults is done in sentences; so let us equip our children to use sentences from the beginning.

TV as a Teacher

Nearly every home has a television set, and most of them project images in color. Used judiciously, television can be a developmental aid in your child's learning. Even a very young infant of four months will respond to the motion, color, and sound. Exposing a well-propped infant to short periods of television will stimulate his sensorial responses. In this mechanical age a toddler often memorizes commercial jingles before his nursery rhymes. If television stimulates him to further learning, well and good. Several factors should govern a child's television viewing.

- One important consideration, of course, is that he must be in a comfortable, safe position. We tend to strap our babies into infant carriers and place them on the floor to protect them against falls. However, it is a rare home that has a television set with the screen at floor level. Thus the babe must surely experience the "front row at the movie" syndrome. Try to place the baby where he can view not only the television but his total surroundings from a comfortable position.

We frequently find our ambulatory children

stretched out on the floor for most activities. Here again, if we provide little rocking chairs for them or permit them to sit on adult furniture, they will be in a better position for viewing. Whatever the age of the child, keep him the recommended six feet from the screen.

- A second consideration is that the length of viewing time should be limited. To use television as an opiate for our children is just short of a crime. How tempting it may be to use television as a baby sitter or as the only source of mental stimulus for our children, but how wrong it is. An occasional program of special interest or beauty is a source of enrichment; a steady, nonselective diet is a tragic waste of these wonderfully fertile developmental years.

    As parents we must exercise control over what our children see on television. It is as much our responsibility to monitor their viewing as it is to keep their immunizations current. Used for an occasional worthy program, television can truly aid in a child's mental growth, but allowance of a child's indiscriminate and prolonged viewing has a seriously negative effect.

Other Sensory Opportunities

Many homes have record players of some kind. Play records often and softly. At times put on a record just for children and include the baby in your family's listening.

- Make sure that if there is a narrative, the narrator articulates clearly and slowly. Here again, discretion must be the watchword. Too much and too loud are conditions to guard against. It is much more effective to play the records quietly.

These children are stimulated sensorially with the parquetry.

- A variety of music is also recommended. A child will respond to a sonata as well as to a heavily rhymthical record, although he may exhibit his responses somewhat differently.

A child who receives sensory stimulation in all areas and from a variety of sources is receiving reading preparation. Reading requires very specialized perceptual abilities and high visual and auditory acuity. The better trained the senses, the better the chance for success in reading.

Books and More Books

Help your child acquire an interest in books and a curiosity about what books contain. Most authorities (Heins 1980) advocate reading aloud to a child from the time she is six months old.

- For children of all ages, choose books that are
  brightly illustrated.

- The content is not as relevant to a baby of six months
  as it is to a two-year-old. Still, it is desirable to get in
  the habit from the beginning of choosing suitable
  subject matter.

- Point out objects in story books to your baby and
  your young child. As she is able, let her identify
  objects in books for you and relate something about
  them from her observation and imagination.

- Part of the benefit of early reading aloud to a baby
  and a young child comes from the physical contact.
  Cuddle your child as you read and create as warm
  and pleasant a time for book sharing as possible. One
  positive step toward reading success is her feeling that
  books are associated with a pleasurable time. At first
  the companionship and feeling of security are the
  most salient aspects of reading aloud to your infant,
  and these feelings carry over into a warm feeling in
  general about books and the act of reading.

- As your toddler's vocabulary increases, let her "read"
  to you by describing the pictures in books. Try to
  select books that are illustrated clearly and colorfully;
  the extra cost is well worth it. Also select books with
  bold print and few words per page. Make books
  readily accessible to children.

- Many babies tear and chew books; so wait until this
  phase is past, but thereafter provide the child with
  her own little library corner somewhere in the house
  where she is free to take whatever books are there. Do
  not underestimate your child's interest in looking at

illustrated books geared for adults. Once she has demonstrated that she will look carefully, do not make your books off limits to her.

- Permit your child to observe you reading. With a toddler underfoot, you cannot, of course, find much time for uninterrupted reading; but there are such times. So let him see *you* reading. Children are natural imitators, and this is one habit worthy of imitation. Some fathers enjoy holding their children as they relax with the evening paper. This, too, can

The little girl is deriving pleasure and utilizing her exposure to books.

be a time of companionship and closeness,
depending, of course, on the disposition of the child.
Maybe your child does not care to sit still while
Daddy reads.

- Perhaps there are older children in the household
  who can read. They will profit from the practice of
  reading aloud, and the younger child will profit from
  sensing that "big" brother or sister enjoys reading.

Speak the Speech Properly

We have already established that baby-talking to an
infant and young child can be detrimental. The proper
kinds of communication are most beneficial.

- First of all, really *talk* to your baby and your children.
  Many of us make negative most of our remarks to our
  children. "Billy, don't do that again." "Susan, put
  down my purse." Of course children need discipline,
  and an overly permissive attitude toward a child is
  often detrimental. But we can emphasize the positive
  and use an upward inflection in our tones at least
  part of the time. Instead of a "No, no, Mama slap
  hands" exchange, we can just as easily use a short,
  complete sentence. Our English grammatical
  structure is complicated enough without our adding
  to it. This does not mean that you must use verbiage
  or make your sentences unduly complex. Simply use
  common sense in your exchanges with your child.

- Occasionally a young child will develop a lisp or
  some other speech impediment that is rather
  appealing. Frequently he outgrows this on his own,
  but it is not always the case. We should not
  encourage this speech peculiarity, however endearing
  it is. Often we can pronounce the words carefully for

him and soon he will make the correct response. However, speech therapy is a specialized area and is not for amateurs to practice. Thus if a speech difficulty persists, consult your pediatrician and follow his advice if he recommends a speech evaluation. The earlier speech therapy begins, the sooner it can come to a successful end. Speech is very important in learning to read, not in merely pronouncing words but in learning to differentiate among sounds, digraphs, blends, and other speech and sound combinations. And we all know that children can wound other children with their blunt questions to a child about a handicap.

- Hearing is vital, of course, in a child's development, but it is possible for a child to go for years with an undiagnosed hearing problem. There are several clues to identify the hearing-impaired child, but often they are so subtle that we ignore them or fail to recognize them.

Station: Checkpoint. Here are a few general checkpoints to observe in your child.

1. Does your infant start at loud or sudden noises even if the sound comes from a distance?
2. Does he respond to a watch ticking near his ear?
3. Does he turn his head to follow your voice even at a young age?
4. Does he give indications of earaches by pulling at his ear or crying his "pain cry" with a cold?
5. Does he jabber at the age you reasonably expect him to, especially the sound of /d/ and /m/?
6. Is his language development within the range of normal guidelines for his age?
7. Are his voice tones gutteral or indistinct?
8. Does he seem inattentive if he cannot see you?

These are only the broadest, general areas in which to observe a child's auditory development. Do not panic if you observe what appears to you as an abnormality. Simply watch your baby or young child, and if you have *any* doubts, let your pediatrician make an evaluation. Some children become such skillful lip readers that they mask their hearing difficulty for a time. Often we scold a child for inattention when, in reality, he has not heard. Or we admonish him to turn down the record player, radio, or television set when he cannot hear it at a lower volume. Hearing difficulties can be remediated, but again the earlier the diagnosis, the more successful the treatment.

■ A difficult thing is being objective about one's own child. Parents are not alone in having this problem. Mates are not often objective about each other, and in most relationships where feelings are involved, this is a problem. But please do look carefully, closely, and unemotionally at your child before beginning your home reading task. Keep objectivity your keynote as you evaluate progress.

Recently I had occasion to observe informally two children playing together for an hour or so. One child, a boy, had turned three within the week. The other child, a girl, would be three in about six weeks. However, I knew I could not contemplate readiness activities for the boy in any formal way at this time. He had a small speaking vocabulary and used almost no sentences; the lengthiest of those was three or four words. He was constantly in motion and exhibited little regard for verbal discipline.

What seemed desirable in this instance was to talk to this child, give him object names, point out and explain simply as many different ideas as possible. He needed a broadened experience with language in general and a firmer discipline in particular. In six months or a year this child might be ready to begin a more formal approach to readiness.

On the other hand, the little girl showed a highly developed language level. She used sentences of six to eight words, explained quite clearly ideas she had, concentrated on a task for several minutes, and was a mature child. If she had been my child, she would have begun immediately on a developmental reading-readiness program. This child gave every indication of being ready.

The point of the above illustration is not to imply that boys are slower in language areas than girls but that the child himself determines a logical starting point. Do not assume that age is the sole determinant. You can properly start a child not yet three, or you can wait until he is six. However, you must not wait to begin all the informal readiness work discussed earlier in the book. Talking to your child, reading to him, broadening his experiences, being consistent in discipline—all these activities are aspects of indirect preparation for reading. With this sort of background, your child should do well in his reading program.

Other Readiness Activities

You can use every experience with your child to lay a solid foundation in language. This does not mean that you must prepare a lesson plan in order to go for a walk with your child. Do not complicate occasions that should be fun!

- However, when you do go on an excursion with your little one, make it a time for sharing. If she is ambulatory, plan to proceed at her pace. It is unwise to rush against the clock when you are walking with

a young child. She cannot keep up physically with
your pace, and both of you will end up tired and
frustrated. Instead, go out with the idea that this is a
time of recreation and relaxation. Remember that the
same amount of ground must be covered on the
return trip. Take time to stop to really look at the
leaf that captures your child's attention. Touch the
snow or scamper after the squirrel. You can talk
quietly with your child at this time. Point out objects
by name, feel them, listen to them, mention the color
and shape of what you see and touch. If she is too
young to verbalize her thoughts, you can do it for
her. "Oh, what cold, cold snow!" is enough to help a
very young child begin to associate names and
properties with objects. Here, again, much of the
learning experience at this point is in the sharing and
companionship.

- Both parents can get in on the readiness act. Father
  can let the little one watch him wash the car and
  permit her to feel the water. Make short explanations
  as you work. The important thing is that the infant
  or the toddler is learning that language and
  communication are linked.

- If you are a mother who is regularly out of the house,
  find a sitter who will carry out your plans for child
  rearing. When you choose your sitter, you select
  someone you can feel confident will tend to your
  child's physical needs. This is not enough, however;
  for these early years are too important to leave to
  chance. Listen to your sitter talk. Does she use proper
  grammar and a varied vocabulary? Is her voice clear
  and loud enough to be audible but not overly loud?
  How many other children will she care for while your
  child is in her care and what are their ages? Will the

television set be the main source of stimulation for your child, or are there books, pencils, crayons, and records for her to share? These are a few of the questions you should have answered to your satisfaction before entrusting your child to a sitter's care.

- The same questions should apply to nursery schools. Merely keeping your child from harm, feeding him, and regulating the temperature are not sufficient care. Cleanliness is essential, yes, but so is proper mental stimulation. Selecting a nursery school will not be included in this chapter, but do make your own careful, thorough investigations. The recommendations of others should not be your only guideline.

- A mother needn't feel guilty about being a working mother provided she is certain that her *total* child is cared for and that she has sufficient energy and good humor left over to share with her child. Dinner preparation can be an exhausting, hectic time, or the returning mother can share this time with the child by putting her in a safe place nearby and talking to her as she cooks. Both parents and child can find this a relaxing, sharing time. Or perhaps Daddy can spend this time reading to or talking with the little one if Mother needs a bit of time to work alone. Family dispositions differ, and each family unit must recognize and build on its own strengths. Perhaps Dad does the cooking and Mom can use this time with the child.

- Some of the most valuable learning experiences for a child can come from relatively cheap, simple things. A trip to the zoo can prove most didactic. What a natural place to discuss animals in general, to point out differences and similarities, to wonder aloud, and to talk. Most little children become very excited over zoo animals, and if there is a group of domesticated animals that she may touch, allow her to do so. Remember that to a city child a calf may be as wondrous as an elephant.

- A trip to a farm is another effective way to broaden vocabulary and to deepen concepts. Always make sure that safety precautions are observed closely, but let your child ride on a tractor and push a wheelbarrow. If she is old enough, elicit her observations and share in them. If she is very young, you can point out casually what you want her to note.

- Conversely, excursions to the city are equally thrilling to the country child. Plan to stop and look at sky-scrapers and streetlights. Ride in a streetcar or a taxi. Use your own judgment as to how much your child can assimilate. Trying to see or do or absorb everything at once is neither possible nor desirable.

- Many teaching materials are at hand. In teaching your child colors, get out the cake-coloring bottles and let him choose the color to tint the frosting. Blue cake tastes the same as white. Another simple project is to give your three-year-old several packets of flower seeds to chose among. Perhaps he can select two, stimulated by the color on the package. Plant the seeds and nurture them together and watch them grow. Not only is he learning color, but he is also making choices and having a most graphic nature-study lesson. As a hint, when you offer your child a choice of the flowers, for example, be sure that the

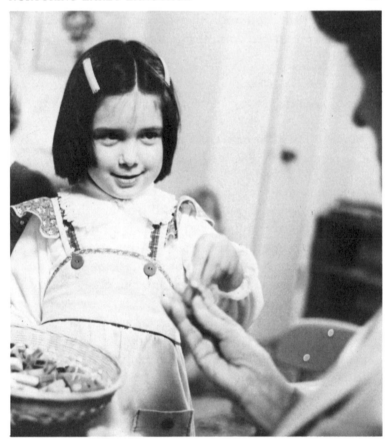

This girl is practicing classification of objects as she hands to the adult an item she has requested. She is also using the grasp that will transfer to writing.

possibilities are reasonable. Choose varieties that are easy to grow in your particular region.

Selecting Toys

A number of instructional toys are available currently. (See Appendix 3.) Select from these materials with care. A child can enjoy a learning toy as much as (and more than) one with mere entertainment value. Shop with the age of your child in mind and also his

level of coordination and other developmental areas. A
toy that is either too complex or too simple will stay on
the shelf.

Do It Yourself

Many household items can be used to give your little
one pleasure as well as instruction (Gray 1948).

- As soon as you *know* he will not put buttons in his
  mouth, provide a muffin tin and perhaps three or
  four kinds of buttons, several of each kind. Show him
  how to separate the buttons according to kind first.
  Later he may classify by color or shape or size. You
  can use the same material still later to count singly,
  by twos, and so on.
    Follow the Montessori maxim of a wordless
  demonstration. Place the muffin tin and buttons in
  some accessible place, and when your child exhibits
  interest, demonstrate one use of the material as
  wordlessly as possible. Then bow out and allow the
  child to use it. Let him discover the possibilities.
    What does such an exercise have to do with
  reading readiness? First, it is accentuating visual
  discrimination—a prerequisite to reading. If a child
  can see a difference between two similar buttons, that
  is a *start* toward discerning differences between /b/
  and /d/, for example. Second, he is learning to
  attend to a task, just as a high level of concentration
  is necessary for reading. Third, he is practicing
  manipulative skills between eye and hand, and this,
  too, is an important factor in reading and writing.

- You can do the same sort of exercise with different
  kinds of nuts in season. This time you might vary the
  practice by using rough and smooth nuts only; thus

you are stimulating the tactile sense. Children delight in the different texture of objects.

- Get out those scraps of materials, Mother, and provide two samples of each kind. Let your young child pair the squares of materials; let your older child match the fabrics blindfolded, according to the way they *feel*. Again, the child is not only receiving sensorial stimulation but is also becoming more aware of his total environment.

- Another toy effective for language development is the telephone. Most children delight in phones, and an infant soon learns to jabber into a soft plastic one. Take time occasionally to carry on a telephone conversation with your child. You can simulate using

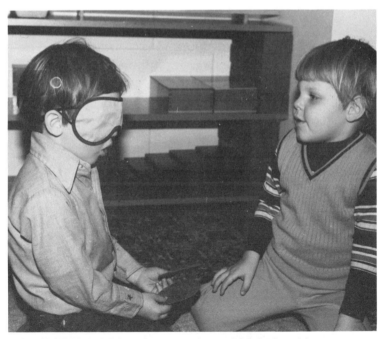

The blindfolded child receives two pieces of fabric from his partner. The purpose of this exercise is to develop tactile sensitivity.

*Large sheets of newsprint and primary-sized colored pens permit
children to unleash their artistic imaginations.*

a phone, or perhaps he will have two toy phones. Not
only does this encourage him to talk, but it is also an
excellent opportunity to teach a bit of telephone
etiquette.

■ A number of satisfactory clays are on the market, but
you can prepare your own simply and cheaply. The
following recipe makes a clay that does not stick or
become difficult to pick up off the floor or table. You
can make it any color you want.

Mix together 2½ cups flour, ½ cup salt, and 1
tablespoon alum.

Mix together 2 cups boiling water, 3 tablespoons
cooking oil, and food coloring.

Combine these two mixtures, knead, and store in a
covered container.

Give your child a hunk of clay and some cookie
cutters of various shapes and let his imagination go.
Ask him questions about his modeling, and thus

carry on a conversation with your child that will result in a natural fun situation. This exercise also results in visual discrimination, eye-hand coordination, and shape differentiation.

The possibilities for teaching your child in these general ways are as varied as your interest and imagination make them. You neither want nor need to program constant learning activities for your toddler and young child. Many of the best learning situations arise spontaneously from what you have planned already as a family.

Perhaps the best advice for you to follow is to talk to and with your child from the first time you cradle him in your arms. Use proper grammar in a soft, loving tone. Let your facial expressions help convey word meanings, and provide him with a variety of stimulating experiences. Let these suggestions become habitual, and you have laid an invaluable reading-readiness foundation.

CHAPTER TWO

The Montessori Way

Language experience and reading readiness do not
end ever. Even as adults we continue to grow and
develop in these areas. However, when your child is
very young is not the time to begin a specific course of
action to teach reading. Again, it is not my intent to
have every preschool child reading, and it is ludicrous to
suggest that your eighteen-month-old will read because
you have invested in this book. However, some children
will be reading before their formal education begins,
and the following chapters are devoted to a step-by-step
approach to reading instruction.

Some words of caution are in order from the very
beginning. The first is that you must not be frustrated
by less than complete success. Remember, anything that
is easy for oneself to do seems easy for another person to
do. But you have been reading for years. Look at a page
written in a foreign language, or, better still, look at
something written in another sort of script. This
language is as strange to you as English words and
characters are to your child.

I must pause a moment here and discuss briefly

Maria Montessori's attitude toward and experience in
children's explosions into reading. In the first *Casa dei
Bambini* or House of Children, Montessori provided the
didactic materials we shall discuss later. Few of the
materials were designed *specifically* for reading. The
emphasis rather was on the manipulative, auto-
educative devices that fostered coordination, auditory
and visual discrimination, observation, and other
readiness areas. Indeed, Montessori herself was startled
when several of the four-and-five-year-olds exploded
into writing and reading. She graphically describes the
scene in many of her works.

Italian, of course, is nearly purely phonetic. This
means that a letter character consistently makes the
same sound wherever it occurs. Thus one does not find
such inconsistencies of sounds as one does in English.
This makes Italian an easier language to read than
English or German, for example.

However, approximately 86 percent of the English
language is phonetic, providing an ample background
from which to approach reading.

Just as one does not throw an infant nonswimmer off
the deep end, one does not present a book to him to
read. Logical, sequential steps lead to the act of reading.
Before we begin to build, however, we must have a solid
foundation. The Montessori approach emphasizes
phonics; therefore, this book leans heavily on the
phonics structure (Olson 1958).

It is not the purpose here to delve into the debate
over various reading programs. A short summary of
some of the most used methods is found at the end of
the book. I believe that a well-balanced approach to
teaching reading at the primary level is desirable;
however, here we are discussing the approach one can
use with the preschool child.

Before considering what materials you will need, sit

back and get ready to review phonics. Some of you will protest, "But I never had it to begin with," or "I never could learn those rules anyway." There was a time when phonics was a dirty word, and many children received no instruction in that area (Botel 1968). Others were bored unutterably by memorizing "rules" for which there were more exceptions than examples. Neither of these is a healthful reading situation. We are not going to mention rules at all to these young children. Neither should we to school-age youths. Instead, allow them to observe and come to their own generalizations. Use an inductive, Socratic approach.

Phonics? Review!

What we shall do in these next few pages is review *one* sound for each letter and *just one* sound. This is what your child will be learning. Ready? Begin.

Aa—this says ă as in *cat, rat, at, mat*
Bb—this says *b* as in *book, baby, boy, ball*
Cc—this says *k* as in *cat, carton, corn, cut*
Dd—this says *d* as in *doll, day, door, den, din*
Ee—this says *eh* as in *set, pet, let, enter*
Ff—this says *f* as in *far, fish, fork*
Gg—this says *g* as in *guitar, get, go, gone*
Hh—this says *h* as in *hush, hope, horse, hot*
Ii—this says *i* as in *it, ill, ink, if*
Jj—this says *j* as in *jump, jug, juggler, jar*
Kk—this says *k* as in *kitten, kite, king*
Ll—this says *ll* as in *lamp, light, limb, lid*
Mm—this says *mm* as in *mouth, may, mop, man*
Nn—this says *nn* as in *no, not, new, never*
Oo—this says ŏ as in *ostrich, not, osprey, ocelot*
Pp—this says *p* as in *pup, pet, push, put*
Qq—this says *kw* as in *quit, quick, quiet*
Rr—this says *rr* as in *rat, right, raw*

Ss—this says *ss* as in *snake, saw, seen, sit, sat*
Tt—this says *t* as in *top, tip, tap, tub*
Uu—this says *uh* as in *up, under, umbrella, udder*
Vv—this says *vv* as in *violin, vintage, vine, victrola*
Ww—this says *w* as in *well, witch, wish, we*
Xx—this says *ks* as in *exercise, x-ray, excoriate*
Yy—this says *y* as in *you, youth, young*
Zz—this says *zz* as in *zebra, zoo, zone*

Please note that only one sound appears for each
letter. Also the sample words are not all vocabulary for
young children. These words are examples for *you* as
adults. Do not confuse the issue by inconsistency. It is
quite enough for your child to learn one sound at first.
Later with experience and maturity he can perceive the
exceptions. Do not push your child! It is far better that
he learn *no* reading from you than that he be "turned
off" to reading in general. You as parents have the
potential of kindling the spark into a lifelong flame or of
extinguishing the glow perhaps forever.

Thus you must learn your lessons well and realize
that there are no magic formulas or instant successes.
Now that you are properly frightened and ready to quit
before starting, settle back and prepare for a good time
with your child.

After you have learned thoroughly the sound value
for each letter, the hard but rewarding part comes in
teaching this to your child. At what age do you start
him and how?

Readiness Checklist

■ First, look at the child objectively. Is he at least 2 or
2½? Rarely is a child younger than this ready for any
formal instruction.

■ Second, is he quite verbal? That is, does he use a

variety of words and speak in complete sentences? Can he phrase a question? If you answer "no" to either of these questions, continue the suggestions offered earlier to broaden his base of experience and facilitate language development. Do be objective in your evaluation of your child's ability. If he is not ready at this moment, wait three or six months and survey again. Because some children are highly verbal at 2½ does not mean that a child who is not so verbal is less bright. Some children flower suddenly and later.

- Third, will your child be willing to sit for instruction for any length of time? This does not mean that he must sit with hands folded for thirty minutes or longer. However, it is necessary that he be able to sit and be attentive for a few minutes. Again, if your child is not ready today, wait a while and try again. If he exhibits some readiness, give it a try. The results may amaze you.

  Children do like a regular schedule, though they are quite flexible, too. Try to plan a time for instruction when you can feel relaxed and unhurried. It may require five minutes initially and expand to thirty as you progress. Do not use a stop-watch schedule, however; be sensitive to your child's moods. Because he spent fifteen minutes, delighted, with the mystery bag on Tuesday does not mean that he is ready for fifteen minutes on Wednesday. Let the time be fairly unstructured, but be aware of your objectives and how to accomplish them. This will be easier if you have a fairly regular time for your presentations.

Select the Best Time and Place

- Select the time when your child is fresh and alert.

A prepared reading corner enhances the effectiveness of the early reading program.

Usually this means after a night's sleep or a nap.

- See that he is not hungry or otherwise uncomfortable.

- Make it a time when you are almost certain to be free of interruptions. A ringing telephone, a crying baby, or other disruptive influences break into the mood and the harmony of the situation.

- Choose a time other than your child's favorite or habitual activity. If he watches Captain Kangaroo each morning, allow him to continue to view one of the most worthwhile programs for children. Of course, you have to decide when he can stop an activity to come to your "school."

- Select the reading corner carefully. You will need a place to put your teaching materials and, if possible, some space for display items. The area does not need to be large, but it should have some permanence if possible. Use whatever system is best for you in keeping your young toddlers from disturbing the older child's materials. Of course, you may well be working with the youngest child in your family. If you have a four-year-old and the 2½-year-old exhibits an interest in what's going on, give it a try. Use your own judgment as to whether the younger child is really interested.

Do We Group?

Another possibility is to include a few other children with whom your child gets along well. The older the children, generally the larger the group can be. Perhaps you might pool resources, two mothers making the materials and one mother doing the instructional work. The main thing to consider is how this affects the child

Small groups of children and cooperating adults offer an effective arrangement.

or children involved. Be flexible and objective in your planning and approach. Do not start out with good intentions, then turn neighborhood participation into a "kaffee klatch."

■ Use your enthusiasm to generate your child's positive approach toward the project. Prepare your materials well and be aware of how to use them properly. Feel confident in your abilities. You have not become a reading teacher. You are rather a parent who is quite interested in your child's learning processes, and you are in a position to do much good for your child.

■ If you get overly tense and exacting in working with your child, consider working out a cooperative program with your neighbor and trading children or groups of children. Again, do this only after much planning and preparation. Make sure that personalities, interests, and attitudes will jibe.

■ If you expect any sort of success in a home reading-readiness program, be consistent in your approach and establish continuity. You must either go all out and work hard or give it up. Whatever time and place work best in *your* situation are the time and place you should use.

Now that you have selected your school corner, have found the appropriate time, and have decided whether to include other children in the group, you must start preparing your readiness materials.

Of course, you have been doing readiness work from birth, and didactic materials are already available to your child. But the materials in the following discussion pertain to Montessori materials.

A number of books on the market describe

Montessori in the home and give instructions on home construction of the Montessori didactic materials. Most of these homemade materials fall short of the beautiful engineering of commercially made Montessori materials; this is to be expected. But the home-constructed materials are useful nevertheless.

This book will not include a set of directions for the construction of any Montessori didactic materials other than for those used *directly* in reading preparation. The towers, cylinders, insets, and many other materials one finds in a Montessori school are aids in the *indirect* preparation for reading, and this is not an attempt to minimize their importance. Yet the materials listed below are much easier and less expensive to construct than the hardware materials.

Sandpaper Letters.   First on the list of requirements are the sandpaper letters.

- Find out from your local school system what method of manuscript writing is taught, that is, whether it is Palmer, Zaner-Blouser, or some other method.
- Obtain a copy of the capital and small letters that your child will learn. You can usually acquire these from a kindergarten or primary teacher, perhaps in your neighborhood school. Use these letters as your models for letter formation.
- If you do not feel talented enough to cut and paste your own sandpaper letters, most large cities have school supply houses that carry such items, retail. If you prefer to make your own, color code them with vowels on blue board and the consonants on red. The board can measure approximately six by four inches, and it should be of a durable material, such as plywood. Each board will contain a single

Sound boxes are both fascinating and didactic.

letter made of sandpaper pasted firmly to the board. Use a medium-rough to rough grade of sandpaper because the child's tracing of the letters with the fingers is very important. The letters should be formed as perfectly as you can possibly make them.

Sound Boxes.   A second didactic material is a *sound box.* Start saving your shoe boxes or boxes of a similar size. (They are easier to store if they are uniform in size.) You will not want to wait until you have purchased thirty to thirty-five pairs of shoes before you begin preparation. Borrow from friends, relatives, neighbors, or any other source.

■ Now, assuming you have the necessary boxes, cover with paper any writing on the ends of the boxes.

- On the end of one box carefully print a capital /A/. On the other end print a lower case /a/. Do the same with each letter of the alphabet. At this point do not worry about the blends and digraphs you will present later. The twenty-six letters are sufficient for a beginning.
- After you have assembled and labeled the boxes, begin filling them with objects beginning with the appropriate *sound*. Please note the emphasis on *sound*, not letter. For example, in the /a/ box, you may want to include a model antelope, anteater, antenna, apple, anchor, and other objects beginning with the same sound. For the /b/ box you can put in such objects as a book, ball, balloon, box, bonnet, buffalo, bank, boy, and so forth. These are only a very few examples of the possibilities. The idea here is to provide as many different objects as possible that begin with the same sound. Use a large variety and make them as explicit and colorful as possible. It is good to include objects that are unfamiliar as a means of vocabulary development. Be sure that the sound boxes include objects and not just pictures.

Some sounds are quite easy to find representative objects for. Others are more difficult, so start looking now and continue your search. You will want to add new items occasionally. Look around you for very easily attainable items. Because you have young children, check the toy boxes for suitable objects. Artificial fruit and flowers are colorful additions. Check novelty shops, variety stores, and your own storage areas. For a minimal amount of money and a maximum amount of ingenuity you can fill the sound boxes with a variety of interesting objects.

As a word of caution, be discriminate in your selections and make sure that each object represents only one sound and that it represents the sound clearly. Also have enough objects so that you can vary them from time to time as you review.

Mystery Bag.   A second didactic material is the *mystery bag*. As you will learn shortly, this item is not only valuable in your reading program but it is also useful in stimulating all the senses. The mystery bag should be as attractive and eye-catching as possible. Use materials such as velvet or a less expensive imitation, brocade, or a psychedelic print. Sew the material into a large pencil-bag shape measuring about 18 by 24 inches and put a drawstring elastic closure in the top. For one who

The mystery bag is an alluring item from which a blindfolded child randomly draws an object to identify by touching.

who does not sew, trade a favor with a friend or involve Grandmother.

Before you begin your use of sound exercises, use the mystery bag for sensorial enrichment and vocabulary additions.

- Assume you intend to emphasize the olfactory or smelling sense. Fill the mystery bag with several objects that have a variety of odors. You might include a lemon, a cinnamon bottle, some onion flakes, a flower, and similar objects.

  After you have filled the mystery bag with these scented objects, invite your child to play the "mystery bag" game. Blindfold him and invite him to reach into the mystery bag and take something out and smell it. After he has investigated the odor, ask him, "What do you think you are smelling?" If he cannot identify the item by its odor, suggest that he feel it or shake it. Occasionally a child will object to a blindfold; in that event, suggest that he close his eyes tightly and playfully admonish him not to peek. Usually after a short time most children are quite receptive to a blindfold.

  Let him guess at all the objects and then remove the blindfold to allow him to see which ones he knew. Try to include one item that will be unfamiliar to him in order to acquaint him with something new.

  You can start the use of the mystery bag when your child is quite young. However, do use judgment in the number and difficulty of the items. A child must experience success to develop self-confidence; so do not defeat him with impossible tasks. As his age, maturity, and range of experiences broaden, you can fit the challenge accordingly.

- The mystery bag can be used as a gustatory or tasting experience, an auditory experience, or a tactile one. Often a child will use a variety of senses in identifying objects.

- Use the mystery bag only occasionally so that the level of interest in it remains high. Keep it in a closet and take it out when you have time to use it with your child.

- The way one uses the mystery bag as a reading readiness aid is to place in the bag objects beginning with one particular sound only. For instance, if you are studying /f/ you might want to use such items as a *f*unnel, a *f*an, a *f*ish, a *f*awn, and others. Use the same procedure of blindfolding and drawing out items for your youngster to identify as you use for sensorial exercises.

Please note that it is a single sound only that we emphasize initially; therefore be careful in choosing objects that do *not* begin with blends. For example, do not use *f*lag as an object beginning with /f/. Save that item for your blend work later. Bombard your child with a variety of objects beginning with the same sound so that he does not associate only one item with a particular sound.

Sound Cards. Now that you have prepared the sound boxes and the mystery bag, it is time to turn your attention to the preparation of *sound cards.* You construct these materials by pasting pictures on poster board. This work requires time in that you must find pictures that are clearly defined. Use large, colorful, uncomplicated pictures so that the emphasized sound is clearly discernible. Magazines are a source of pictures; the produce department in supermarkets may let you

Sound cards are a keystone in the early reading program. Note the possibilities for using the language experience approach and for imparting general knowledge.

have some of their display pictures of fruits and vegetables; and school supply houses usually have suitable sound-card materials.

The poster paper can be of different sizes, depending upon what you write below the picture. As you begin your sound work, keep the writing to a minimum. Center the picture on a card about 18 by 18 inches and print the capital letter on one side of the picture and the lower-case letter on the other. Then print carefully two or three sentences, using words with the emphasized sounds as frequently as possible. One sound card per sound is insufficient; use a number of them.

The sound cards are an excellent way of adding to knowledge because you can print an entire informative story about a picture on the card. For the /j/ sound you might paste a picture of a baby kangaroo called a *Joey*. By using several sentences you can emphasize the /j/

sound and simultaneously talk about this interesting baby animal.

A useful rule of thumb is to keep the sentences short and simple in relation to the child's age and background level. Again, variety and quality should be the key. It is better to have fewer sound cards and have excellent pictures and carefully written sentences.

For example, you might use the following. *Sound:* short vowel /A/ /a/. Use a plain, very realistic picture of an apple.

- *For a beginner: A*nn h*a*s *a*n *a*pple.
- *For a more mature child: A*nn h*a*s *a*n *a*pple. She c*a*n h*a*ve it *a*fter lunch *a*s a sn*a*ck.

   (Note: Do not worry about using the indefinite article /*a*/. Children must learn to recognize this as a sight word when the letter stands alone.)

- *For an advanced student: A*nn h*a*s *a*n *a*pple. It is so shiny and red. *A*nn's d*a*d h*a*s a b*a*sket of *a*pples *a*t home. *A*fter dinner *a*t night *A*nn and her d*a*d h*a*ve *a*n *a*pple *a*s they read their books.

In the last example, there is one word, *read,* in which the letter /a/ doesn't take the short vowel sound. If the child asks, merely explain that letters make different sounds. Later you will explain about the silent letter in *read.*

English is approximately 86 percent phonetically true; therefore a child must learn early that he or she cannot depend exclusively on a single sound/symbol association.

Let us look at another example of a sound card, using the consonant /*b*/.

- A first-stage sound card might have the picture of a book. *B*ob has a *b*ig *b*ook. *B*arbara reads a *b*edtime story.

- A more advanced card might read: A *busy baker bakes a batch* of cookies. *Books* are fun to read.
- A still more advanced card might read: *Both boys* and girls read *books* as they get older. *Babies* enjoy picture *books but* they cannot read yet.

These are merely examples to show you some possibilities for sound cards. Keep the guideposts in mind but do allow your creativity and imagination to work for you.

A further suggestion is that animals, plants, and other environmental features are usually very popular sound card items. Again, you can offer the sound card and allow the child to dictate his own story, challenging him to use the stressed sound as often as possible.

You will find after doing several of the sound cards that you become "picture oriented" and that as you look through magazines, books, and newspaper color sections, you are seeing pictures with an eye toward their sound-card use.

Perhaps, on occasion, you will want to buy a series of pictures that school-supply houses have available. This may be a group of color pictures on animals, plants, or other objects. And, of course, remember that suitable pictures for some sounds are difficult to find, as the /x/ will demonstrate rapidly to you.

There is no need to panic at this point in the face of what may seem much work. Do not be discouraged, either, if you are not a good printer or if you are not clever at seeing appropriate pictures. Likely you have a friend who likes that sort of activity. For example, if your printing is not good, perhaps you can trade three hours baby sitting for comparable printing time by your friend or bake a loaf of bread to exchange for some cards.

Be sure to use capital letters only as they are appropriate normally. Do *not* use all capital letters.

Discuss the big and little letters incidentally from time to time and this will rarely present a problem to a child.

Now let us review a bit about the state of our reading-readiness program. Your little girl has received many broadening experiences of a sensorial and language nature. She is continuing to be exposed to these sorts of stimuli, and you feel that her verbal ability and attention span are at a level at which you can begin a more formal approach.

You are preparing sound boxes, a mystery bag, and sound charts and are feeling confident that you have the time and patience to continue the reading-readiness program. Perhaps you have planned to include another child or two in the sessions: this you have done after considering the idea carefully. Remember that although some children respond positively to a little healthy peer competition, others need larger doses of self-confidence before competing with others. The time of day is suitable to all concerned, and you have a place for your supplies. At this point you are ready to begin. One word of caution: make this fun and low-key!

CHAPTER 3
Presentation of Material

This chapter deals with the actual presentation of the material to your child. No two children respond alike to the same situation. You must adjust to individual differences.

Let us assume for the sake of a starting point that you have a three-year-old son who is average—if this is possible—in ability. Be honest now, and do not assume him to be precocious. And do not become discouraged if he catches on more slowly than you feel he should.

Expect to spend about a week on one sound, using about fifteen minutes each day for this activity. Again the time guidelines are flexible. If your child is engrossed in what you are doing, spend a few minutes longer. Occasionally children get fidgety; so quit before the interest has abated. You can force your child to be attentive physically, but you cannot compel his mind to learn if the interest is not there.

Tracing the Sandpaper Letters

You and your child are ready to begin.

■ Initially present him with the sandpaper letter and

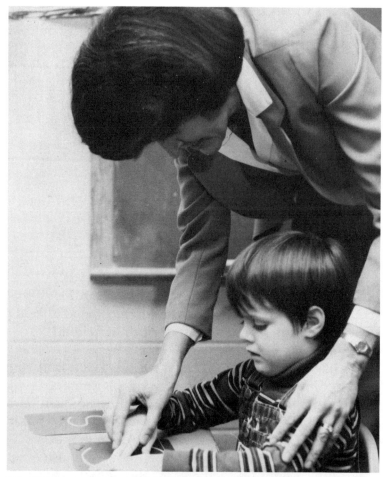

*The directress or parent guides the writing fingers as the child traces
the sandpaper letter.*

invite him to trace the letter. Be sure that he uses the
index and middle fingers to trace, for these are the
fingers that will hold the pencil later. Guide his hand
and say with him, "This says /m/; this says /m/."
Give the letter *sound* rather than the letter name: *m-m-
m.* After he has traced the letter two or three times
with you, allow him to trace it alone. Be certain that
the tracing of the sandpaper letters is done according

to correct configuration patterns. If you are unsure, check your penmanship guide.

Always keep in mind that this is new territory for your young explorer, and it does take time to cement this sound/symbol relationship in your child's mind.

■ Another word of caution may be necessary here: permit your child to establish his own dominance or "handedness." Granted, it is a right-handed world, and right-side dominance makes it easier; but do not force it. A disagreement is current among reading authorities as to the importance of lateral dominance in reading development; so do not try to convert your child toward right-handedness. Watch to see which

Note the total concentration as the young learner traces upper- and lower-case letters.

A favorite exercise consists of removing from the soundbox objects that all have the identical initial sound.

hand he consistently prefers to use in tracing the sandpaper letters. The three-year-old may be a "switch hitter," but by four or five he will usually use one hand exclusively. A simple way to make an informal assessment of hand dominance is to place an object on a table before him and invite him to pick it up. Do this several times to see which hand prevails. Or hand several items to him one at a time to observe again with which hand he reaches outward.

A child is especially receptive to any sensorial stimulation, as Dr. Montessori pointed out; thus the tactile or touching exercises involved in tracing the letters stamps letter formation on his mind. And the younger this experience occurs, the more profitable it is for your child.

Using the Sound Boxes

In conjunction with presenting the sandpaper letters, get out the sound box filled with the items beginning with the sound you are teaching. Let us continue with /m/ for purposes of example.

■ Open the box and remove an item from it. Give it to your child to hold and explore. He may respond immediately and say, "Oh, look at the monkey." You can answer, "Yes, this is a *m*onkey and monkey starts with /m/." Each time that you say the /m/ sound, emphasize it. Remember to use letter *sounds,* not letter names.

■ Continue in this manner through several or all of the items in the sound box. If his attention wanes, tell him to go play and that you'll have fun again tomorrow. Probably you will find that as you go along his attention span will increase and the sessions can last longer.

Practicing with the Mystery Bag

The next day present the same sandpaper letter again and ask him to tell you what the letter *says.* Do not be disappointed if he cannot recall the sound today. One day he will be able to.

■ Ask him to trace the letter again two or three times and say, "This says /m/."

■ Take out the mystery bag and, with him blindfolded, let him delve into the bag and select something. See if he can identify it by touching, smelling, listening, or using any of his other senses. After a short period of time for exploration, if he cannot identify the object, remove the blindfold for visual identification. Reinforce the idea that this is a *m*an, for example, and *m*an starts with /m/.

- Continue in this way through three or four items from the mystery bag.

- Close out the session with an oral repetition of the sandpaper letters. It is preferable to stop while the interest is still there rather than to exhaust him.

Using the Sound Cards

Before you start the third day you will want to put up some of your sound charts, making sure you use the most explicit of them. This will be a new device to catch his attention and to emphasize this particular sound. On the third day get out the sandpaper letters again for him to trace and repeat aloud.

- Ask him to look about the room to see if he can find any other letters that say /m/. You hope that he spots those on the sound charts. If he does not, point out the symbol and ask him to tell you what it says. Hold up the sandpaper letter if necessary next to the sound chart, directing the child to trace the sandpaper letter and repeat the sound of the letter.

  Please remember that it is not catastrophic if he cannot recognize an /m/ elsewhere or tell you the sound. This is just the first rudimentary step toward reading. Success does not occur overnight.

- Read the sentences on the sound charts aloud to him, emphasizing words beginning with the /m/ sound. If he has picked out the /ms/ on the sound card, ask him to underline each letter that says /m/. It is exciting to a child to participate in the learning situation as much as possible. He will feel important as he marks on the charts. Be sure that you guide his hand from left to right under the letter. At every opportunity, establish the left to right, top to bottom sequence.

- If he has not singled out the /m's/, leave the underlining for another day.

These first three days will have acquainted your child with the essential idea of the sound/symbol relationship, and the ice will be broken. Assess your presentation very carefully and objectively and evaluate ways in which you feel you were either successful or need more practice. Keep in mind that this is a slow-building process and that it will appear very mysterious until you have participated actively in helping a child get ready to read. The pressure is not on you to send your child to school reading. Compare your situation with the early primary teacher who must produce results en mass. When this cannot be a joyous experience for you and your child, stop to discover why. A positive set toward learning in general and reading in particular is a far more important outcome than his learning to read in the preschool years.

- The fourth and fifth sessions of your presentation for the week will be more of the same. Use your mystery bag, sound-box, and sound cards but vary the items. If he has selected three items earlier from the mystery bag, take those out and let him select new ones this time. The procedure is the same, and the variety is necessary to broaden the concept base, especially in a very young child.

  Usually five days of presentation are sufficient, but the individual child determines how much time is necessary. If he seems to have mastered the concept rather than simply the association by rote, go on. If he seems completely baffled by the whole idea, retreat from it for six weeks and try again.

- You will implement these activities by reading stories

to him, preferably those relating to the stressed sound.

- Perhaps with his modeling clay you can make one or two items beginning with the emphasized sound and point out that he can make them too. Do not become overly didactic, but take advantage of each opportunity as it presents itself.

Second-Week Activities

Now that you have reached the second week, you may be ready for a second letter. It is better to choose your letters out of alphabet sequence in order to build toward a stock of letters sufficient for writing phonograms. If your child can recognize a number of commonly occurring consonants, the vowels can fill in a bit later, and you will be at the phonogram stage. A second consonant might be /t/.

It is desirable initially to use letters that are less frequent causes of speech problems and are not as confusing configuratively. As you practice saying /m/ and /t/, for example, you will note the very different speech formation of those sounds. Thus, less possibility exists of confusing two such differently formed and pronounced sounds.

Week two continues in the same vein as the first week. By now possibly a pattern is emerging that will help you to help your child most efficiently. After he perceives even vaguely the whole *idea* beyond a sound/symbol relationship, the rest of the steps will be easier. Be patient. The majority of children do perceive this idea sooner or later.

Presenting Vowels

Another wise investment at this time is a set of alphabet cards *without* illustrations for the letters. The rationale behind the nonpictorial cards is that occasionally a young child associates a particular symbol with one whole word. For example, he may reason that the figure (or symbol) /A/ says *apple* rather than concluding that /a/ says /a/ and apple starts with /a/. (Be sure to use only the short vowel sounds at first.) Put up the alphabet card as you present each sound. Again, if you do not use a sequential presentation, you will likely create a firmer understanding of each letter.

- Build a stockpile of several consonants such as /m/, /t/, /s/, and /f/.

- After these are well in mind, proceed to a vowel. As a suggestion, start with /a/ since its sound generally creates less confusion. Do not worry about any other sounds for the letter /A/ other than /a/ as in *a*pple, *a*nd, *A*ndy, and so forth. You will have much time later to go into various vowel sounds. It is not necessary to distinguish at this point between vowels and consonants. Your sandpaper-letter backgrounds are color-coded, remember, and this is sufficient. Casually you can mention it, especially where younger children are concerned.

- It is important that you keep reviewing sounds; do not assume they are printed indelibly in your child's mind even after he appears to have them well learned. Make your review a game. Get out the sandpaper letters you have covered and tell him you are sure that you can fool him. Every one he identifies correctly, he gets to keep, and each one that he misses and *you* know, you can have. Say you'll count them at the end. Flash them to him, not too rapidly, of course, and make a point of his getting more letters than Mommy!

- If this is not the case, and your child seems genuinely uncertain or confused, you can see that you need to go back and do more work. If this backing up is necessary, go through the same procedures you used in the initial presentation. Do try to vary the sound cards and objects, however. This is sound practice to keep interest sustained. It also emphasizes the idea that one sound can occur in many words and that wherever it does, the sound is constant.

- What if your child is confused in general and either does not know the sound/symbol relationships you have presented or is obviously guessing? First, observe his attitude closely. Is he distressed at sensing or knowing he is wrong, or is he "pulling your leg" today? If he is concerned, reassure him as thoroughly as possible and put the work away. If he is amusing himself by giving wrong answers deliberately—and your child will do this—tell him when he is ready to work to let you know; then simply sit there impassively for a few minutes. This may sober his attitude so that you can continue, or he may be unduly excited about something and unable to settle down. In that event, merely put the work away and dismiss your child. Beware if this happens often, and take gentle but firm steps to eliminate undue clowning during lesson time; this can carry over into formal school. However, the approach of Christmas, a birthday party, or some other big event can account for loss of attention. Strike a happy balance between too much frivolity and too much soberness. If you note your child's becoming nervous or feeling unduly pressured, back off in the intensity of your approach. The object is to foster a love of reading, not the reverse.

Teaching with a Calendar

While all this is occurring in your developmental program, you may also want to buy a large calendar with removable numerals, a slot for the month, and one for the year.

- You can help give your child some time-orientation by filling in each date as you come together for the daily lesson. Such an exercise helps build vocabulary—words such as the ordinal numerals *first*, *second*, *third*. Teaching the concept of extended periods of time is usually difficult. The main purpose for the calendar is language development, but time-sense development can occur also.
- The holidays in each month are areas that invite discussion. Each season has its own joys to anticipate,

The boy, using Woods Reading Drawers, matches phonogram-type words to the stimulus pictures.

and you can help set the stage for these by talking about the coming first snowfall, for example. You can say and point out that "this is March, and March starts with /M/." Do not be surprised if your child comes to recognize visually the names of the days of the week and months of the year.

On to Phonograms

To continue with our reading program, let us assume that your youngster is recognizing and associating the sound with the letter symbol in all the letter-sound combinations that you have presented to him. You have several consonants and the vowel /a/.

■ Now present the vowel /e/. Do so with great care, for a similarity exists among vowel sounds that can be confusing to children. You will not find quite the variety of objects for /e/; so choose carefully and work with patience.

■ After your week spent on /e/, go back and review.

When you feel your child is about unshakeable on sounds, the phonogram step is next on your reading-readiness program. This step can well be one of your most gratifying experiences, for if your child can unlock phonograms, he can be reading soon.

■ Use a small blackboard or flannelboard and flannel letters. Either will suffice, but at first perhaps a blackboard is preferable. As an example, let us use the word *man*. It contains the letters you have presented and is a familiar word to children.
  ■ Write a lower-case /m/ on the board and elicit from your child what the letter says. He will reply with the /m/ sound.

- Leave a bit of space and print /a/ on the board, again asking him to respond with the proper sound.
- Finally do /n/.
- After he has given the three correct responses in isolation, explain to him that now you are going to put these sounds together, and they will make a word that he can read. Write the letters as a word now and touch under each letter asking him to say the sounds.
- Now show him verbally how to elide the sounds quickly enough so that a word emerges. Some children at first find this rather hard to do. Remember, the concept of reading itself is entirely new to this young child. If he does not seem able at this point to make the word from its sound components, go over it again and show him. Ask him to listen to you and then to tell you the word you have just said. Suggest that he close his eyes and listen hard. When you say the word this time, sound it slightly more emphatically and more slowly than you say the word normally. Perhaps he will hear *man* and say it. A correct response warrants enthusiasm on your part as it is a significant step. Patience is the watchword with the child who still does not hear the word. Do work with him until he can hear *man* from the sounds that you say even if you have to say it nearly outright.
- Suppose your child decodes the phonogram immediately? This is a tremendous achievement, one that deserves a praising comment.
- Suggest now to him: "We can change this first letter and make a *new* word." Erase the /m/ and put /t/ in its place. See if he can decipher *tan* on his own. If not, help him sound out each letter,

then elide them into a word. If he does pronounce
tan on his own, make a praising comment and say,
"Let's read another word."

- This time put in /b/ or any other consonant that
will form an actual word with the ending *an*.
- Go through as many of these as you can, stopping
either when your sound supply is exhausted or
your child loses interest. However, the latter is
unlikely to happen if he is decoding spontaneously.

This business of sounding and saying phonograms is
significant. It means that the child is forming accurate
sound-symbol relationships, that he can synthesize
them, and that the process comes across to him as a
meaningful word. It is definitely a step toward reading
success.

Do remember, please, that this program emphasizes a
phonics approach and that phonics is only one aspect of
reading. I feel that for young children it is a sensible,
logical beginning point. Again, approximately 86
percent of our language is phonetic, and a child can get
off to a worthwhile start from such an approach to
reading.

- For the child who seems cognizant of the particular
sound for each symbol but who cannot yet synthesize
them into words, back off and present more sounds.
If he continues to develop in this area, wait a month
and try phonograms again. No two children have the
same developmental rate, and the slow starter of
today may leap forward tomorrow. Again, do not
become concerned or "pushy." You are laying an
invaluable foundation for reading success.

- Continue your program with the child who is reading
phonograms. Each day becomes a bit fuller as you

introduce new sounds, do calendar work, and write phonograms on the board.

- At this point put up a word that he can read and ask him to tell you a story about it.
- Write down sentences as the child dictates them so that he can see words flow into sentences.
- Read back to him what he told you, then ask him to come underline all the words that begin with some particular sound. Perhaps he can spot some simple words that he volunteers to read on his own.
- Vary this approach as he increases in ability to read phonograms. Put up simple sentences using three phonograms. An example of such a sentence is "Tom can sit." Be sure to use capitals and periods as needed. A bit later you can point out these punctuation marks rather offhandedly. A child who is reading these short sentences is well away indeed. It is an excellent beginning, but you can do more in your home lessons.
- Do not expect a child who is not reading phonograms fluently to read sentences. A toddler does not become a distance runner overnight. Continue to present sounds to him, review frequently, do lots of reading to him, and keep it fun! One day there will be an "explosion" into reading that will delight your child, not to mention you!
- Few books for children are written from a completely phonics structure; so be judicious in choosing at the library. Often a child wants to try his newly discovered skill on books of all sorts. This is excellent, of course, but you must keep him reassured that there are many words that he cannot read and that no one expects him to read every word yet. Thus, when you journey to the

library, help him select books that he wants you to read to him or books that are well illustrated so that he can tell about them.

- Keep right on through all the letters of the alphabet. Possibly with constant tracing of the sandpaper letters he will want to try writing the letters. Let him suggest this to you, however. Many children in the prepared environment of the Montessori schools do begin printing on their own. However, they have had the further advantage of all the didactic materials related to preparation for writing. In fact, in the usual Montessori situation, children write before they read.

- If your child exhibits an interest in printing, obtain some lined, primary manuscript paper and make a pattern for a particular letter with small, numbered arrows drawn in to emphasize letter formation. Help him to form the letters properly from the start. The paper may prove too restrictive. If so, give him larger, unlined sheets. But the letter shaping should be done properly. He can scale the letters down in size later. Much of the success or lack of success here comes from the level of coordination development and the opportunity the child has had to work with didactic materials that foster writing activities.

Movable Alphabet

Still another recommended material is a movable alphabet that can be of either the wooden or plastic variety. (Cardboard usually is not as durable as you want the product to be.) It is even possible to use the magnetic letters that come with some children's blackboards or pegboards. Preferably, the consonants should be red and the vowels blue to correspond to the color coding of the sandpaper letters. This color coding

This boy is using the movable alphabet as the next step of his reading.

reinforces the beginnings of his awareness of vowels and consonants.

■ Pictures should accompany the movable alphabet. Keep constantly on the alert for pictures that are easily recognizable and can be spelled correctly phonetically. Often story books, coloring books, the workbooks of older children, magazines, and department-store catalogs are sources for pictures. Begin quite simply with such pictures as a mop, a map, a bottle of pop, a top, and so forth. Later you can increase the complexity of the spelling and the concept; for example, you can select pictures

depicting the word *rock* as both a noun and a verb.
Directness and simplicity are the keys to choosing
pictures.

- The proper way to use the movable alphabet is to
  present the child with five simple pictures and ask
  him to spell the words with the alphabetical letters.
  Remember, this comes only after his mastery of
  phonograms and his ready familiarity with most
  single sounds. Do one of the words with him to
  demonstrate precisely what you mean.

*The same boy is at a more advanced stage in this exercise that teaches
the silent E generalization, the first vowel digraph taught.*

- Choose the picture of a *cat*, for example. Lay the picture out and say to him, "What is this?" He will respond, probably, "This is a cat." Now say to him, "I am going to spell *cat* with these letters. Let's see, I need a /c/," (Use the *sound*, not the letter name—and select one), "an /a/" (and select one), "and a /t/." As you select the letters, put them down in order. When you have finished, read the word. "Yes, I have spelled *cat* haven't I? You may do the next one." Usually the child will delight in working with the movable alphabet.
- Have him tell you what each picture is so that you can be certain he is seeing what you intended that picture to represent. For instance, if he perceives as a kitty the picture you present as a *cat*, the misconception will complicate the use of the movable alphabet for him.

Blends and Digraphs

Now that your young reader is proceeding apace, you should begin work on presenting blends and digraphs. A blend is two or three letters that together form a sound, but each separate letter retains some of its own identity. Examples are *dr, st, str, br, tr, gl*, and so forth, as in *dr*ip, *st*ep, *str*ip, *br*ing, *tr*uck, *gl*ad.

Digraphs are two letters that together form a single sound. Examples are *sh, ch, th*, as in *sh*ip, *ch*ip, *th*is. Please note that the digraph *th* says two different things. For instance we have the word *th*is and the word *th*in. In these words the same digraph makes a different sound.

Blends. Your method of presenting blends will be somewhat different from that of presenting single sounds. When your child has approached the level of maturity that will allow him to do blend work, that is the time to begin. You ask, "How will I know that he is

These children are engrossed in Woods Reading Drawers and the movable alphabet as they master the ck *blend. Movable alphabet vowels are red, and consonants are blue.*

ready?" You may answer that question by asking yourself these questions:

- Is my child completely reliable as to his single sound-symbol relationships?
- Does he work successfully and confidently with the movable alphabet and phonograms?
- Does he seem eager to go further with the reading task?

Your unqualified, affirmative answers to these questions should tell you to go ahead with the blends.

- As the first step, write a word such as *drip* on the board. Ask your child to read it. Perhaps he can do so

without much difficulty. If that is so, try the word
drop next. Continue with blend words for a time until
he either experiences some difficulty or demonstrates
that the presence of a blend in a word does not
present problems to him.

- It will not be unusual if he does have some difficulty
  in synthesizing blend letters at first. Let us assume
  that he does. The first thing you can do is say the
  word that is creating the problem. As you say it,
  underline *from left to right* the blending letters and
  emphasize, for example, the *dr* part of drip.

- Invite him to say the word after you and explain that
  instead of saying *d r i p,* each sound in isolation, he
  will say together the letters you have underlined.

- Go over several examples in this way; then put a
  blend word on the board for him to attack
  independently. Some continued difficulty means that
  you will want to back off from blend work for a time.

Some of you are wondering what four-year-old can
understand all this. Not every one, to be sure, but
remember, we are discussing a child with whom you
have worked for some time—weeks or months. He has
demonstrated to you through his steady progress that he
is ready for such a step.

- You will present sound boxes containing objects
  beginning with blends. Whereas in the /b/ box you
  will have a book, ball, bag, and similar others, in the
  /br/ box you can have a *br*ick, a *br*oom, a picture of a
  *br*idge, and so forth.

- The sound cards will contain pictures and sentences
  emphasizing the appropriate blend.

- Do not teach the blend concept in isolation but rather as a step in the reading ladder. Write short sentences on the board containing single-letter sounds and blends such as an, ant, *b*it, *b*rick. This helps you to note whether he is keeping the sounds sorted correctly in his mind.

The desirable way to convey a reading concept is to teach it in context with what he has already learned and to allow the child to draw his own conclusions. Thus, if possible, use many examples, involve your child fully, and do as little explaining as possible. Answer his questions about letters and combinations and sounds

Here the emphasis is on the sh *digraph as it occurs initially and finally. From the phonic spelling of the picture card image, the children progress to writing the words on primary-lined paper.*

simply and clearly. He does not want or need at this point a course in linguistics.

Digraphs. Digraphs are presented in much the same way as are blends. The most common digraphs are *sh, ch, th,* and *ng.*

- Get out the chalk and ask him to tell you as many words as possible that begin with *sh*. He may list *sh*oe, *sh*ip, *sh*op, and others. You write down each word he says, always moving across the board from left to right, top to bottom. When he has exhausted his supply, you suggest several and write those down also.

- Next say to him, "Please come underline the letters that say *sh* in each word. Watch me do the first one, and then you come help." Make a big point of pronouncing the digraph sound in the word *ship*, for example, and of underlining the *sh* together. Repeat the word and draw the line again under the digraph. Then let your child come and underline. Pronounce each word for him and guide him to underline two letters from left to right. After you have helped him with two or three, step back and allow him to work independently. Any time he falters, step forward and pronounce the word, emphasize the digraph, and guide his hand under the letters as he underlines. When the digraphs have all been underlined, pronounce them again and retrace the underlining.

- Next read two or three attractive sound cards; then stop for the day.

It should be a comfort, parents, to remember that you have all the time you need for this work. If he does not perceive it today, you have tomorrow, and no one will withhold your contract or approach you critically. Keep the whole procedure low-key and fun.

- Do a lot of sound-box and sound-chart work with blends and digraphs. Do not concern yourself too much with distinguishing for your child the difference between digraphs and blends. Simply make the presentations matter-of-fact and interesting.

- Saturate your children with examples. *Fish* and *dish* and *ship* are good words for illustrating the *sh* digraph, but they are insufficient alone. You can find pictures demonstrating *shop, cash*, and other less concrete words. The whole project takes effort and ingenuity, but with determination you *can* succeed.

- Use puppets to help cement these various sounds in your child's thinking. One little hand puppet could be "Mr. Sh," and you can concoct a variety of stories as you go along. Children respond to laughter and joy; they learn more readily in its presence.

- Keep alert to the possibilities offered by coloring books or inexpensive children's books. You may find precisely the picture you need from a dime-store book. Substitute ingenuity for dollars.

Look, Say—No Way!

The question of sight words or basically "look-say" reading frequently enters the picture. Many parents take the following approach to "teaching" their children to read. They will buy a book with simple words that they feel the children should know; then they proceed to point out the word in isolation. "This says *dog*—d-o-g, *dog*. Now you say it." Sometimes children do learn a few words in this way by sight recognition, and for those who will experience no reading difficulty ever, it may be all right, or at least not detrimental. But it really does not have much practical application at this point and may confuse the entire issue of reading.

You will ask why many first-grade teachers work to build a stock of sight vocabulary words. First of all, they have done much readiness activity so that the ground has or should have been prepared. Next, using their series as a guide, they present words in light of later reading encounters. Third, having a stock of 50 to 100 words gives a child self-confidence to attack reading with a feeling of success. He is more receptive to other aspects involved with the development of reading skills if he feels he can read.

Please also bear in mind that at first-grade level a child is usually geared to read. For many, reading is their reason for coming to school. Children have a more mature set toward reading at six than at three. You, of course, are accomplishing these same goals for your child, who is younger; but you are working slowly, carefully, and building step-by-step as you go. With one child or a very small group you can back up, you can stay at one level, or you can accelerate, according to your child's need. This is your advantage. Ideally, this would be possible at all levels, but it is more difficult to practice with large groups in public schools.

With the approach you are using with your child, you are teaching him *one* aspect of word analysis, mainly phonics. As he grows in skill at unlocking words, he can read more and more and thus can begin to use context clues, however basically, and to build a stock of sight words.

- He needs to know some pivot words after he is reading independently. Some of these are *the, mother,*

An adult pronounces a sight word for the child.

father, and perhaps a few others. Simply explain that
sometimes we come upon words we cannot sound
out. One of these is the word *the.* This is an abstract
word for a child; so use it in many short sentences
that contain words your child can read easily. Note
that he is at the stage of reading complete sentences
before you even attempt these sight words. The word
is may cause a few problems because the letter /s/
says /z/ in this case. Let him encounter *is* in a
contextual situation and if he decodes it, make no
explanation. If it causes difficulty, give him the word
and see if he remembers it. If he does, make no
explanation unless requested. If he still has trouble,
explain that in *this* word /s/ says /z/. Then use the
word several times in context in the next reading
sessions. The object is not to overemphasize one

particular word; present it so that a child can utilize it in his reading. Perhaps a few other sight words, such as names of siblings, are in order; but do not attempt to build a large sight stock. Your child is very young, remember, and the phonics approach will work quite well. You do not want to confuse the issue by fragmenting your approach.

■ You do want your youngster to reach the point where he can say familiar words automatically. Most reading reaches this point; so do not encourage your child to continue to "sound out" words after he can say them from recognition, from context clues, or from other methods of identification. However, sounding out words is an effective way of decoding a word frequently, and a child feels confident in using the method. You are building this very important link in his chain of reading skills.

■ Word endings can come along in your teaching structure without causing undue stress. Plurals, for example, are usually no major problem because of the many verbal applications for a child. Sound cards are effective tools in conveying the idea of plurals. Talking with your child, too, will serve to get the plural noun concept implanted. For example, have a sound card with one object repeated a number of times. You might find a picture of balloons or horses or kittens or a dozen other objects. In these instances write sentences, using plural forms of the noun. Ask your child to count with you. Usually children delight in counting. Then say, "We counted seven balloons." Emphasize orally the /s/ on balloons. Show him a sound card using a single-item picture. Ask him to count it. Afterward say, "Yes, we counted one apple." Briefly summarize that we say, "one apple" but "seven balloons."

Of course, most children readily assimilate plurals into their speech patterns, but emphasizing it as you read is a subtle way of teaching plural endings. As your child's maturity develops in reading readiness you can simply and offhandedly mention that one thing is called *singular*. More than one thing is called *plural*.

Give him some oral examples: "one cookie," "two cookies," "one bear," "two bears," and so on. Then ask him to tell you his own examples.

With methods such as these children prepare for the act of reading without its being a laborious task. When the transfer comes in reading, accomplish it by presenting many examples in context and with a movable alphabet. Really, you will find that plural forms of nouns probably will not trouble your young reader.

Building Word Endings

What about the present progressive or present participle ending in *-ing*? The method I have found effective is telling the child that *-ing* says *ng*. Technically the letter /i/ should not be included in your digraph, but it seems easier for the child to remember if you make this simple statement. Again, the best approach for cementing this idea is emphasizing many examples. The desirable way of teaching is to allow a child to make the discovery; therefore, give him the framework and permit the youngster to fill it in. At first choose simple verbs that he knows that add *-ing* without doubling the consonant or making other changes. Use such words as *jump, sing, bank, tell* in short sentences; then alter the sentence to use the *-ing* form of the word. As soon as he has mastered this step, go on to the many other words that *double* the consonant, such as *hit, sit, swim, hop, tip, run, dig,* and others. It is not necessary to note to him the orthographic (spelling) change. He may

Increasing sophistication in reading occurs as skills build. This child is pairing identical words with two different pictures. For example, she puts the word sink *by a picture of a kitchen* sink *(noun). She also places the word* sink *by a boat that is about to* sink *(verb).*

question you, but probably he will find the doubled consonant no trouble. Explain carefully to him that when two sounds that say the same thing come right together, he says the sound only once.

This leads to the presentation of such combinations as *-ck* in words like ro*ck,* sli*ck,* sho*ck.* Give sufficient opportunities for him to see and read the words and to work with the movable alphabet. By the time you present the materials of this nature to him, his reading level should be high enough to cope with these complexities. Of course this is the beauty of your working in a relaxed way with your young child. No guideline dictates to you that you must teach certain reading principles by a particular cutoff. Always watch to ascertain that he is grasping whatever concept you are emphasizing. If he is not, back off and try again later.

Vary Activities

A variety of activities to prevent boredom is necessary when you work with young children. One morning make your reading activity consist of a story that he especially likes. Another day let him read to you. Always, however, keep using the sandpaper letters, the movable alphabet, the sound cards, and the sound boxes. Treat the reading time as a happy time. Keep pressure low, but do work. Dr. Montessori observed that the basic nature of a child is to love work, and you will find your child settling down to the reading task if he is adequately prepared.

CHAPTER FOUR
Where to Go from Here

What do you do with your child who seems able to go on into a reading text? Most textbook supply houses do not sell to individuals, and it is difficult for a lay person to choose a program that is best suited for his child's needs.

■ The wisest course of action is to consult a primary teacher in whom you have confidence and ask for her suggestions. Possibly you can buy an individual kit of materials from a school. A satisfactory source of formal reading material is a programmed course that follows a predominantly phonics approach. Nearly every reading program comes equipped with teachers' manuals that may be sufficient to explain the program to you if you study them thoroughly. However, remember that these manuals are designed for use by professional people and that there can be gaps in your knowledge regarding certain terms or procedures. If you have questions, do not hesitate to ask an experienced teacher for an explanation. Stay away from the more innovative approaches such as

When children begin to use reading materials, they are elated. The children in the background are waiting to read with the teacher.

the Initial Teaching Alphabet in your home teaching. These very specialized methods are best left in the hands of the school teacher, partly because of their experimental nature and partly because of the training necessary for the instructor.

- Of course, when your child has arrived at this point in his program, you will want to continue enrichment experiences.
  - Ask him if he wants to write a little story or a letter. He will use a mostly phonic approach to spelling, and punctuation may be lacking; but the idea that he can communicate is the important thing.
  - Give him every opportunity to visit the library or the child's section of bookstores, for he is now well away toward lifelong success in reading.

Checklists

Certain physical factors sometimes impede a child's ability to read. Too much and too little has been said on the subject. Too much has been mentioned in such areas as lateral dominance with too little knowledge of the implications. Too much has been bandied about under the term *dyslexia* without an agreed-upon definition. This term especially appears to be in the *speaking* vocabulary of many and the *meaning* vocabulary of few.

Occasionally parents and teachers will note that a child reverses a letter or a numeral once in awhile and will conclude that the youngster has a reversal problem or a visual difficulty. Many times this is instead a natural course in his development. Strike the happy medium between baseless fear and proper concern. Do observe your child carefully for signs of impending or existing difficulty. If you note a behavior that *might* indicate an eye problem, consult your pediatrician. He

Note the various reading activities that occur simultaneously in the carefully prepared reading area.

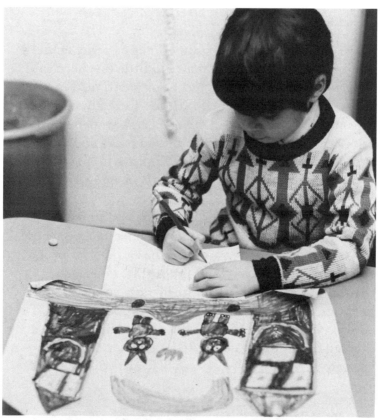

This five-year-old has written and illustrated his own story.

can make the necessary referrals. Do note if your child consistently has trouble in establishing a left to right, top to bottom order or spells aloud to you backwards. For example, does he frequently read or spell *Stop* as *Pots?* Does he squint or close one eye or rub his eyes for no obvious reason? Does he appear clumsy? You can use several informal checklists as you observe your child. It is much better to check and find nothing wrong than to risk letting a physical defect go undetected and untreated. However, do not label your child as a potential reading problem if he reverses a letter once in a while.

Here is an informal checklist you can use to note *possible* physical problems. By *no* means is this a substitute for a pediatric evaluation.

1. Does my infant respond to loud noises?
2. Does my infant follow an object with his eyes by the age of three months?
3. Does my infant perform physical tasks, such as rolling over, standing, and walking within normal time limits?
4. Does my child participate in physical activities at about the same level of coordination as his age peers?

   Note: Be careful in comparing your child at age three with a four-year-old or even a child six months older. Months can make a big difference developmentally.

5. Does my child favor one eye?
6. Does my child have to sit very close to the television?
7. Does my child seem to understand speech better when he looks at the speaker?
8. Does my child pronounce *most* words correctly by age four?
9. Has my child suffered from frequent colds, sore throats, or earaches?
10. Can my child maintain a simple rhythm for several minutes on a drum or other percussion instrument?
11. By age three can he carry out sequentially three simple commands? For example, "Johnnie, please go upstairs, get your shoes, and bring them to me"?
12. Can my child walk the length of a wide balance beam by age four?
13. Can my child toss and catch a ball as well as do others his age?
14. Does my child have a sense of humor?

15. Does my child enjoy being hugged and physically loved?

16. Does my child habitually repeat what is said to him?

17. Has my child made an emotional commitment to a toy, a pet, or a sibling?

18. Does my child handle eating utensils efficiently for his age range? (By age four the child should be able to use a fork and spoon with ease.)

19. Is bedtime *usually* a peaceful time with sound sleep following?

20. Is my child frequently cheerful and responsive under normal circumstances?

Note also that you receive the best performance from your child when he is well rested. This applies to your home sessions and to school later on. Plentiful sleep is requisite to a successful school experience.

Nursery Schools

The value of parents' teaching their child at home versus enrollment in a preschool situation is often asked about. This book is not the suitable place to discuss nursery schools in depth. However, the entire subject is being discussed broadly, and some discussion here will probably neither help nor harm the issue.

- First, you might ask yourself what your desired goal is as a result of preschool for your child.
- Second, you should know about the type, design, and personnel of the preschool under consideration.
- Third, you will be concerned somewhat about the cost factor.
- Fourth, and most important, the child himself and his own needs must carry the most influence in

whether you place your child in a preschool
situation.

The purpose here is neither to condone nor condemn
preschools. Suffice it to say that you can do the task of
reading-readiness preparation—even reading itself—*if*
you are consistent in your approach, patient toward
your child, conscientious about keeping to a schedule,
willing to work hard and imaginatively, and if you are
realistic in your expectations. These are some big *ifs* you
must consider carefully before attempting this job. If
you cannot honestly say that you feel able to go ahead
for any reason, then give the project up and investigate
preschools. On the other hand, if you feel reasonably
secure about the procedures, begin preparations now.
Remember, no teacher ever has a guarantee of success
or any secret formula for teaching reading, and neither
do you.

This small book is not an "open Sesame" for reading
readiness, but the techniques described here are sound
and have worked with many children over a period of
years. They will work for you if you follow the
prescribed methods and uses of materials. The success
you have can be a boost to your child's academic
success, and for this reason you will surely proceed.

However, you may decide that you truly do not have
the time, or you must work outside the home all day, or
for whatever reason you cannot begin a more formal
approach. Then do look into a preschool for your child.
Consider every aspect, including your child's social and
emotional readiness, and make your decision only after
much painstaking investigation. A preschool should be
open for your visits and questions. Ask every question
you have before enrolling your child and continue to
ask them later, too.

The area of nursery school selection is a separate
topic in itself. However, as a guide in selection you

might ask yourself several questions.

- First, what do I as a parent want for my child from a nursery school? Do I want him to have educational experiences or merely competent physical facilities? No school can be all things to all children; so decide on your priorities and evaluate accordingly.

- Second, be absolutely certain that the preschool meets the guidelines of your state. Is it certified for the number of enrolled pupils? The state regulations involve such factors as fire safety features, adequate ventilation, square footage per child, numbers of personnel on duty, restroom facilities, kitchen and eating accommodations if meals are served, outside play space, and health requirements for staff and children. Check out your state code, available from your state department of education, and ask to see licenses.

- Third, talk to parents. Find out whether they are satisfied with their children's preschool, and get details on what they particularly like or dislike.

- Fourth, visit on two or three occasions to make a more valid observation. This will help you determine how consistent the behavior of the staff is.

- Fifth, try to determine whether the enrolled children appear happy, calm, and relaxed. Does the individual child seem to get some special attention appropriate to his or her needs? For example, is the teacher aware of the shy child sitting in the corner?

- Sixth, is the physical environment bright, clean, and child-centered? Is furniture scaled to the requirements of little ones? Are wall hangings such as pictures and mirrors on the eye level of the children?

- Seventh, how long has the school been established? What is its reputation in the community? Is it supported privately or with government funds?

- Finally, take your child to visit his potential school and gauge carefully his reactions. Afterward, talk to him about his feelings if he can verbalize his ideas.

Think the selection process through as objectively and as rationally as possible. There is no excuse for delaying reading-readiness preparation before kindergarten. Parents, preschool teachers, television programmers, anyone connected in any way with young children have this responsibility. Tomorrow is too late to start.

CHAPTER FIVE

Implications of Early Reading

What are the implications of early success in reading or advanced readiness preparation when your child gets to school? You can rightfully ask, "Why hurry up to wait?"

Encouragingly enough, the current trends in reading are toward improved reading series and an emphasis on the individual child. Many schools are beginning to use or are already using ungraded groupings. Briefly this means that a child may be in the second grade and go to fourth-grade reading and second-grade math, or the reverse. These kinds of arrangements—and there are several—are helping to provide answers to the questions of individual differences.

The days of "See Spot. See Spot jump" are also ending, and more systems are turning to new methods of reading instruction. Therefore, your child will find in his formal school experience a variety of approaches— and possibly placement at his ability level. More schools yearly are turning to ability grouping in reading *among* rather than *within* the classrooms.

Administrators and teachers are paying close

Increasingly, reading series are written more appealingly to young children.

attention to the possible ways to help each child read at his maximum capacity, and the child who begins school with a firm readiness foundation has an advantage. Of course, some children start school and read successfully who have never been worked with at home, but these are the exceptions. You need only observe the problems in the inner-city schools that are populated by children from culturally deprived backgrounds.

You can help the situation—and learn from your

experience—by working as a VAIR (Volunteer Aide in Reading) through your local school district. You may also work as a volunteer in a Head Start center. By observing and participating in such programs, you may see for yourself the necessity of language development and early childhood education. In addition, as a volunteer you will be contributing greatly to programs for less culturally advantaged children.

In no way interpret this to mean that material poverty alone guarantees reading problems. It certainly does not; there can be environmental poverty of educational opportunities in the most affluent homes, as well as emotional poverty. However, generally more affluent parents are more concerned with their children's education.

The avenues of approach to reading are many. You have just read several recommendations for general readiness, and the book has outlined a rather specific

Cross-grade grouping can benefit each child involved.

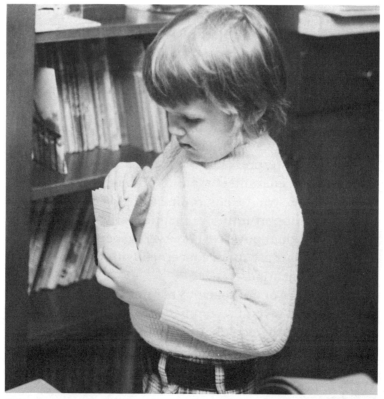

This boy's training has developed to the point that he uses the library check-out system.

instructional program. The materials are not expensive to make, and you can conduct your formal sessions with your child alone or with a small group.

This book emphasizes phonics as a suitable approach with young children because it gives them something concrete and specific to follow. As the child progresses satisfactorily through these steps, a more generalized approach can be used. You are the teacher involved in this home situation, and you can set the pace according to your child's needs, remaining as long as necessary at any one phase. It is also your responsibility to determine how ready your child is to begin this program and to back off for a time if he does not appear to be ready. At all times you can build backgrounds of experience and increase vocabulary.

- Answer his questions patiently. Take him with you to a local shopping center when you do not have to rush.
- Let him see farm animals at close hand.
- Show him city buildings; visit the post office, a fire and police station, and the public library.

Parents can design such a library corner at home.

- Enroll him in the Children's Story Hour popular in most libraries.

- As soon as the library rules permit, let your child have his own card.

- Go camping and hiking with your youngster.

- Attend athletic events together.

- Many communities have puppet shows available for tots.

- If you are close to an urban area, check special children's performances of plays and ballets or concerts. What a rich holiday tradition is attendance at *The Nutcracker Suite.* (If the child is ready for this rich experience.)

Children have little reason to decode words beyond their meaning experience. What possible feedback does a child have if he can pronounce *elephant* while reading but he has no idea what an elephant *is*? Broaden those meanings by providing an enriching range of experiences. Many, many of the best opportunities are free. When you begin to look for occasions to share with your child, you will see more as your own awareness heightens.

The preceding pages have presented numerous ways to broaden your child's horizons. In the appendices following Chapter 4 are still more suggestions for your use as a parent and teacher.

Good luck in your role as reading teacher. Work hard, patiently, and joyously!

The following is a list of phonograms to aid you in preparing your board work. Use only actual words. If a word is not in your youngster's meaning vocabulary, use it and explain it incidentally. This introduction to a word broadens vocabulary and removes restrictions from your using certain words.

at	*ad*	*ot*	*ab*	*et*
bat	bad	cot	cab	bet
cat	cad	dot	dab	get
fat	fad	got	fab	jet
hat	gad	hot	gab	let
mat	had	jot	jab	met
pat	lad	lot	lab	net
rat	mad	not	nab	pet
sat	pad	pot	tab	set
tat	sad	tot		vet
vat	tad			wet
ed	*id*	*it*	*ob*	*ut*
bed	bid	bit	Bob	but
fed	did	fit	cob	cut
Jed	hid	hit	dob	gut
ked	kid	kit	fob	hut
led	lid	lit	gob	jut
Ned	rid	nit	job	nut
red		pit	lob	rut
Ted		sit	mob	tut
wed		tit	rob	
			sob	

At a later time add blends to these roots to make new words. For example, add *gr* to *ab* to form *grab* or *gl* to *ad* to form *glad,* and so on. You can also double the final consonant to make new words and to show that the same sounds occurring together are said only once. An illustration of this is *putt* or *mitt.* Still later try adding a silent letter such as *k* to *not* to make *knot.* The variations on phonograms are many, and most children get the idea of what you are doing rather quickly. The forming and unlocking of phonograms is satisfying to young children because they are actual words, and that means reading to youngsters.

Some materials on the market in the form of games

and flannel-board cutouts may be helpful. Most of these, however, are designed for use with somewhat older children. Look over the material carefully before you purchase it to be certain it meets *your* specific need at this point. For example, Milton Bradley puts out a set of phonetic drill cards called *You Can Read.* This is a source of phonogram material and is an adequate supplementary material, but it uses long vowels also. With your child you probably are not past the short vowel sound. So do be sure that any outside materials you bring in tend to cement rather than confuse your child's concept development. You might come up with your own simple games, such as bingo.

CHAPTER SIX

To the Teacher

It is quite feasible for kindergarten and primary
school teachers to use these same materials and
techniques.

- The language-experience approach continues to be a
  popular method of building prereading and early
  reading skills. The sound charts are ideal to use in
  this activity. Here, perhaps, the teacher would prefer
  to use a picture or a concept to stimulate discussion
  in lieu of a single sound. The child benefits, of course,
  in expressing himself orally. In turn, he observes that
  the spoken word assumes a printed form that conveys
  a meaning to himself and others. Self-expression can
  also become a catalyst for emotions the young child
  needs to vent.

  A language-experience chart story lends itself to
  other areas, such as science or social studies.
  Frequently an idea will grow into a much broader
  concept for the child or children involved.

- Printing children's language-experience stories into

individual books is a rewarding culminating activity.
If the children can print, each can copy his own
story. If that is not possible, the teacher can type or
print individual stories, reproduce them, and bind
them into a personal book. Perhaps the children can
provide illustrations too. This sort of tangible
outcome gives young children added incentive to use
language and to develop the communication skills of
speaking, reading, and writing.

Sandpaper Letters

One method of working with learning disabled
children is the Frenald Method. Very briefly, this
approach involves tracing in sand to heighten sensitivity
to the formation of letters. This, in turn, transfers to
written work at a later time. Certainly sandpaper letters
are appropriate tools in an elementary classroom.

Oral Reading

I remember with joy two elementary teachers who
read aloud to their classes. Before most of the pupils
could read independently, one first-grade teacher read
aloud daily to the class. It became a special part of the
day, this post-lunch treat. The selections represented a
wealth of childhood literature.

The other splendid teacher frequently read poetry
and encouraged choral reading. It was from her that
groups of children learned to read poetry as it was
intended to be read. If early education fosters a love for
the printed word and an appreciation of language, a
major purpose of education is served.

All sorts of reading skills develop from being read to.
For example, a teacher might read part of a story and
then ask, "What do you think will happen next?" This
sort of exercise emphasizes ability to predict outcomes.
Another exercise emanating form oral reading asks
children to fill in words aloud as the teacher pauses,

thus using context clues and vocabulary enrichment.

A child who is listening to oral reading is practicing attention-building skills and concentration, two necessities in reading success. Effective learning techniques that start almost in the cradle continue to be effective tools throughout childhood.

Show-and-Tell Variations

Show-and-tell time is a familiar standby in many primary classrooms. This activity develops expression, group sharing, attention span, and a variety of such positive outcomes.

- When you are introducing a particular sound, present the sound to the student and ask the child to bring an object that begins with that sound and share information with the class. You will be pleased at the inventiveness of these young children in finding unusual objects at home. Not only is the sound emphasized, but also the information shared can be an enriching experience.

- Young children respond enthusiastically to an invitation to add to the mystery bag or the sound boxes. They delight in adding an item of interest that other children can use also.

A happy corollary to any of these activities is the positive attitude children express toward school and learning. As youngsters become involved with their own educational environment, the outcome is more productive.

Educational Games

What often passes for play is really the task of learning in a preschool or primary classroom.

■ Such old-time favorites as "Old McDonald's Farm" and "Farmer in the Dell" are learning experiences. The participants are practicing rapid decision-making (in selecting players), sequencing activities, and memorizing. Under the guise of play, young children are using fundamental reading skills.

■ Children's art and music have been coordinated in many classes. These sorts of experiences can be linked to reading readiness also. Let us suppose that the lesson is to create secondary colors. A good time to introduce this concept is in the autumn when leaves are turning in many areas of the country.

   ■ The instructor can relate colors to sounds to introduce or reinforce a sound/symbol association. Then during free painting time the child can create his own secondary colors, labeling them himself or with your help.

   ■ Afterward, children enjoy very much being autumn leaves and singing "Autumn Leaves Are Now Falling." Such coordinated activities are designed to bring closure to the child's learning experience while providing a variety of linking situations. This type of procedure is easy to follow if one person is responsible for most activities in the classroom. If others are involved, coordination of effort and goals can be achieved with planning.

   ■ Rhythm band instruments are also didactic. Almost all children respond enthusiastically to playing rhythm instruments. In the young child this activity fosters eye-hand coordination, essential for success in writing and other academic activities. They also practice counting while playing, sharpening listening skills at the same time. So often teachers at the preschool and early primary levels are called upon to defend much of

These stimulating materials help children conceptualize even as they have fun. Many readiness tasks are performed with these didactic items.

what they do. Yet even the seemingly most simple activities are building essential reading skills.

- Children, even nonreaders, can benefit from dictionaries and sets of *Child Craft,* for example, as well as editions of children's publications, such as "Jack and Jill," "Ranger Rick," and "Humpty Dumpty," among others. Additionally, children learn to handle their own and others' books and magazines with care.

- PTAs and other parents' groups often have funds available to buy items for the classroom. Teachers are excellent sources of suggestions. Requested items are frequently books; but aquariums, rhythm

instruments, extra art supplies, phonographs and
records, living plants, sound boxes, and other such
objects are excellent gifts to the classroom.

The exciting thing about a variety of stimuli is that
often a child's interest is whetted. This spurs him on to
find further information even at a primary level.
Frequently such interests will become lifelong and, with
a ripple effect, lead on to more and more curiosity and a
generally heightened awareness of the world around.

What About the Early Reader?

Parents, school board members, and others often
seem to feel that if a child enters school reading, he will
somehow have problems.

As teachers you can allay those concerns. Of course,
you who are daily in the classroom have observed
repeatedly the readily apparent levels of children's
reading. Some pupils learn rapidly and advance
steadily; other youngsters progress much more slowly
and less evenly. Within weeks great differences have
emerged. This process occurs whether children have
reading skills developed at three or at six. You must
individualize, and you do need grouping under any
circumstances; so why worry that some children are
more advanced? It is the children who lag behind that
generally create concern.

Once the general public understands that vast pupil
differences occur in almost any classroom, perhaps they
will fear "accelerated" reading less. It seems part of the
professional task to answer such concerns.

The day is surely coming when few primary-age
children are held at a certain level because "that's first
grade work for next year," or "that's third grade work
and you are only in second." Few educators still teach
in that vein; soon, we hope, there will be none. To be

meaningful, curriculum must be designed to meet students' needs. It must be responsive to new knowledge of the learning process. The days of static lock-step education are buried.

Still More Activities

As children acquire decoding skills, they enjoy using this new ability at every opportunity. An activity youngsters delight in is using command cards. Initially there may be only one word on the card. For example, the child can draw a 3- by 5-inch oak tag card from a stack of such cards. One card may say *run* while another card may say *jump*. Later, as more sounds are mastered, the cards can contain such brief sentences as *"Shut a book"* to longer sentences later on. An incidental outcome is the observance of whole-sentence punctuation and capitalization.

Teachers may also divide a group of children into teams, allowing each side to count points for the child who reads his card correctly or obeys the command first.

The amount of progress determines the complexity of the command cards. Later entire short stories can be printed or typed on cards for children to enact.

References

Botel, M. 1968. *How to teach reading.* Chicago: Follett
  Educational Corp.
Gray, W. S. 1948. *On their own in reading.* Chicago: Scott
  Foresman.
Heins, E. L. 1980. From reading to literacy. *Today's
  Education* 69 (April–May):41G–46G.
Jennings, F. G. 1973. *This is reading.* New York: Bantam
  Books.
Kohl, H. 1973. *Reading, how to.* New York: Bantam
  Books.
Morphett, M. V., and Washburne, C. 1931. When
  should children begin to read? *Elementary School
  Journal* 31 (March):496–503.
Nila, Sister Mary, O.S.F. 1953. Foundation of a
  successful reading program. *Education*
  73(May):543–55.
Olson, A. V. 1958. Growth in word perception abilities
  as it relates to success in beginning reading. *Journal
  of Education* 40(February):25–36.
Smith, H. P., and Dechant, E. V. 1961. *Psychology in
  teaching reading.* Englewood Cliffs, N.J.: Prentice-
  Hall.

Suggested Reading

Caplan, Frank, ed. *The Parenting Advisor.* Garden City, N.Y.: Anchor Press/Doubleday, 1977, 569 pages.

This large volume is a compilation of viewpoints from 800 books on childrearing. The topics cover nearly every aspect of a child's life. Especially informative are Chapter 8, "Language Acquisition", Chapter 9, "How Do Babies Learn"; Chapter 10, "Play and Playthings"; and Chapter 14, "Enrichment Activities." The book also contains addresses of educational material supply companies and a discussion of numerous toys, games, and books. The entire contents are presented interestingly and provide a current, valuable source of information.

Gordon, Ira J.; Guinagh, Barry; and Jester, R. Emile. *Child Learning Through Child Play: Learning Activities for Two-and-Three-Year-Olds.* 4th ed. New York: St. Martin's Press, 1972, 116 pages.

This small book contains a number of games and activities for the young child. Most or all of the ideas presented can be utilized from very common household materials. Each activity described has a stated developmental purpose. There are also a number of simple illustrations.

Harris, Robie H., and Levy, Elizabeth. *Before You Were Three*. New York: Delacorte Press, 1977, 144 pages.

This is an interesting book, beautifully enriched with over 100 photographs of infants and young children. The thrust of the book is an explanation to two-and-three-year-olds of their physical and emotional development. Adult readers gain a novel insight into the world of the very young. While the material is somewhat superficial, the book contains enough depth to be of value to parents.

Larrick, Nancy. *A Parent's Guide to Children's Reading*, 4th ed. New York: Bantam Books, 1975, 374 pages.

Larrick has written a thorough, informative guide for parents. Of special interest for parents of young children are ideas to foster early language development. Other strengths of the book are the sections "Buying Books for Children," "Tools for Book Finding," and "Books They Like." There is also a list of publishers, recordings, filmstrips, and films. For these practical considerations *A Parent's Guide to Children's Reading* is a handy source book. One drawback is the way in which Larrick disposes of early reading without a fair or proper research treatment.

Montessori, Maria. *The Child in the Family*. Chicago: Henry Regnery Company, 1970, 120 pages.

The small book presents in a concise way much of the Montessori philosophy toward children and education. This highly readable, warm book should be on the reading list of parents and teachers who want an introduction to the Montessori approach.

Singer, Dorothy G., and Singer, Jerome L. *Partners in Play*. New York: Harper and Row, 1977, 205 pages.

This practical book demonstrates the necessity of play in a child's total development. An especially applicable chapter is "Living and Playing Through All Our Senses." Several games are described, as well as the practical use for each activity. Lists of recommended books and records for children and an adult reading list provide further useful information. This book is of value for preschool and primary level educators, as well as for home use.

Travers, John, ed. *The New Children: The First Six Years*. Stamford, Conn.: Greylock Publishers, 1976, 165 pages.

This paperback book is a scholarly, research-oriented book that emphasizes the effect of early experience on the child's development. Topics covered range from the "Multiple Functions of Play" through "Special Learning Problems of Young Children." Despite the academic cast, the book is written in a straightforward way and contains much material of value and interest to parents and educators.

APPENDIX ONE
Montessori Exercises

Exercise in Packing a Lunch Box

The activities in this appendix are taken from my Montessori notes. These are developmental exercises that can be used by parents at home or by preschool or elementary-level teachers. Each activity fosters specific skills directly related to reading readiness or to other communication areas.

Materials:
A basket or a lunch box, a place mat, a napkin, a plastic mug, a thermos, a small bar of soap and a wash cloth in a plastic bag, a sandwich, nuts, fruit, and milk.

Presentation:
Assemble all materials on a table. The sandwich is wrapped in foil or waxed paper. Nuts and sweets are in a small container. Milk is in a thermos. Pack first what is to come out last. Take care that fragile foods are not crushed.

Purpose:
Development of foresight and planning and a sense of the science of dietetics.

Point of interest:
Choice of wholesome foods.

Control of error:
When removed, the articles are in the order of use. Materials are left in their original position for the next person.

Age:
Any preschooler.

Rough and Smooth Touch Boards

Materials:
Four boards, each 6" x 8"
1. Divided into two equal parts, one smooth and one rough sandpaper.
2. Divided into alternate strips of rough and smooth.
3. Divided into six rough surfaces, from rather rough to very, very rough.
4. Divided into rather smooth surfaces to very smooth.

Presentation:
1. Hold board in one hand.
2. Stroke evenly with the first two fingers (used in writing). (Movements should be light and delicate.)
3. Speak softly, saying, "This is rough." "This is smooth."
4. Take next board in hand. Stroke as before, saying "Rough." "Smooth."
5. Take next board in hand. Stroke as before, saying "Rough," "er," "est."
6. Take next board in hand. Stroke as before, saying "Smooth," "er," "est."

Purpose:
To develop tactile sense and to control muscular action by lightness of touch.

Point of interest:
Finding roughest board.

Control of error:
No error is possible.

Classification of Nuts

Materials:
1. Quantity of mixed nuts, at least 6 of each kind:
   Walnuts
   Almonds
   Brazil
   Filberts or Hazel
   Pecans
   Chestnuts
   Cashews
   Peanuts
2. Small tray
3. Container for each kind of nut
4. Basket

Presentation:

The children are invited to come to the table where the nuts are. The teacher sits at the table and gets help taking the nuts from the basket and mixing them.

After each nut is discussed and named, the children are told to classify the nuts into groups called families. Stress real and unreal by using a real nut and an artificial nut. Incidentally, review rough and smooth concepts with the nuts. Explain that walnuts are so called because at one time they grew up a wall. Try to tell a story about each kind of nut used. Pass the nuts around so the children may feel the nuts. Halves and wholes are easily taught with a walnut because the halves are so easily defined.

A child may choose a kind of nut to classify. Write the name of the nut on the board. The child then puts all that particular kind of nut into a cup. Stress that nuts are a kind of fruit.

Return the nuts to the original container and mix them so they will be ready for the next child.

The children may be blindfolded to do this exercise. Stress the word *classification.*

Purpose:

To teach the tactile sense and a better knowledge of fruits.

Control of error:

1. Visual discernment.
2. Tactile discernment.

Fabrics

Materials:

Two pieces of many different kinds of materials, such as silk, cotton, satin, corded silk, chiffon, cheesecloth, wool, felt, velvet, corduroy, denim, pellon, nylon, dacron, cotton lace, taffeta, burlap, and others.

Presentation:

The teacher names each kind of material. A child is invited to match one kind of material.

The children do this in turn until all the materials are matched and named.

The children are encouraged to feel the material while learning to name it.

The children are blindfolded, or they close their eyes and name the materials blindfolded, using only their sense of touch (tactile sense).

The teacher discusses each kind of material and gives such information as whether the material is animal or vegetable.

Silk: animal—made by silk worms.
Cotton: vegetable—grows in fields in warm climates.
Satin: mostly silk—therefore, mostly animal.
Chamois: animal—from Himalayas.
Cheesecloth: cotton—vegetable.
Wool: animal—from sheep.
Felt: wool—therefore, animal.
Velvet: mostly silk but partly cotton.
Corduroy: cotton.
Denim: cotton—used for hard wear.
Pellon: used for interfacing.

Purpose of lesson:
1. To learn the names of fabrics.
2. To improve the optical and tactile senses.

Point of interest:
1. Seeing so many lovely fabrics.
2. Feeling the differences (rough, smooth, soft) in the fabrics.
3. Being able to match the fabrics correctly.

Control of error:
Only two pieces of each kind of material; they must match.

Mystery Bag

Materials:
A beautiful bag filled with articles (five senses, A to Z).

Presentation:
1. Teacher takes out each item and places it on a large table.
2. Teacher elicits name or tells name of items. Teacher includes
   some of the following:
   Auditory: ear
   Olfactory: smell
   Gustatory: taste
   Tactile: touch
   Optical: eye
   Stereognostic: touch plus feeling

Purpose:
1. To review alphabet.
2. To review five senses.

Point of interest:
Anticipation and participation.

Control of error:
Visual.

Reading

Reading readiness is found in the system of writing readiness.
1. Left to right sequence.
2. Sandpaper letters and composing words with movable alphabet.
3. Phonetic boxes and word placement.
   a) Loose word cards under the objects.
   b) Didactic ladder sequence.
4. Phrases and charts: letter studied for the day used in repetition to increase knowledge by sound as well as sight.
5. Command cards (comprehension tested).
   a) Acting out a single-action word.
   b) Acting out a phrase.
   c) Acting out a sentence.
6. Phonetic readers or chalkboard study.
7. Vocabulary building constantly increased by phonograms.
8. Books, books, and more books.

Making Butter

Materials:
1. One-half pint of cream.
2. A cold jar with a tight fitting lid.
3. A glass for the buttermilk.
4. A plate for the butter.
5. A knife or a spoon for removing the butter.
6. A towel for cleaning up.
7. Paper napkins on which to serve the butter and crackers.

Presentation:
Pour cream into the cold jar and tighten the lid well.
Ask each child to take a turn shaking the jar vigorously until the butter forms.
Hold back the butter with the spoon or knife while allowing the buttermilk to pour into the glass.
Place the separated butter on the plate and shape into an oblong.
Use the towel for cleaning up any mess.
Ask each child to spread some butter on a cracker for himself.

Point of interest:
1. Each child participates.
2. The children listen to the butter forming. From a liquid comes a solid and a liquid.
3. Butter comes out yellow. The color depends on the time of year, the feed the cows have had, the type of cows, and many variables.

4. The buttermilk is poured off the butter.
5. Each child is able to spread, taste, and eat the butter he has helped to make.

Purpose:
To study how butter is made and to see natural sequence.

Control of error:
1. The lid must be screwed on tightly.
2. The cream must be shaken long enough.
3. All buttermilk must be poured off the butter.
4. Be certain to have enough butter for each child.

This is exposition. The same plan can be used for making many things: cakes, bread, puddings, and others.

Timetables for Speech Sounds

Age in Years	Sounds Mastered
3½	b, p, m, w, h
4½	d, t, n, g, k, ng, y
5½	f
6½	v, th (as in *th*at)
7½	z (as in azure),
	sh, l, s, z, r,
	th (as in *th*in), wh

APPENDIX THREE
Manufacturers of Stimulating Toys

Blocks and other unstructured toys that encourage fantasy are preferable. Here the recommendation is for sturdy wooden blocks.

1. Childcraft Education Corp.
   20 Kilmer Road
   Edison, N.J. 08817

2. Fisher-Price Company
   200 Fifth Avenue
   New York, N.Y. 10010

3. Playskool
   P.O. Box 8243
   Church Street Station
   New York, N.Y. 10049

Rhythm instruments can be ordered from:

1. Childcraft Education Corp.
   21 Kilmer Road
   Edison, N.J. 08817

2. Children's Music Center, Inc.
   5373 Pico Blvd.
   Los Angeles, CA. 90019

3. Creative Playthings, Inc.
   Edenburg Road
   Cranbury, N.J. 08512

Stacking Toys ("Big Bird" and "Oscar the Grouch"):

1. Child Guidance
   1055 Bronx River Avenue
   Bronx, N.Y. 10472

2. Playskool
   P.O. Box 8243
   Church Street Station
   New York, N.Y. 10049

Building Sets: Playskool Village, Tinkertoy, Crystal Climbers, Bristle Blocks, Blockmobiles: From Playskool (see address above).

Toy telephones: Be sure that these are sturdy; buy two so that each converser has one. These are available in almost every toy department.

To order Montessori materials in the U.S.A.:
   Nienhuis Montessori USA
   320 Pioneer Avenue
   Mt. View, California 94041

Components of a Prepared Environment

1. Use child-size furniture and utensils where possible.
2. Provide low drawers and closet furnishings easily usable by the child.
3. Decorate his room to scale by placing pictures, lamps, and book shelves on his eye level.
4. Use plants, flowers, shells, and other natural objects to stimulate a child's visual sense and appreciation of beauty.
5. Play "good" music by various composers and musicians.
6. Use soft tones in speaking to your child; encourage *listening*.
7. Teach your child to keep his home or school orderly.
8. Foster care of possessions, his and others.
9. Provide a variety of illustrated books for the child.
10. Insist on task completion if the child possibly can do so.
11. Consult your child in making decisions that pertain to him. (If there is a choice between a red or blue sweater, let him decide.)
12. Appreciate beauty, harmony, and love of learning yourself; then communicate these feelings to your child!

Woods Reading Drawers

Series I and II are a systematic, sequential way of teaching a phonics approach to decoding and encoding words. Each skill is reinforced constantly as a new skill is presented. These materials are available to parents and are also used in several public and private schools and in special education classes.

Ordering information: Dorothy A. Woods
210 Meadow Lane
Council Bluffs, Iowa 51501